BATMAN

fortunate son

WRITER
gerard jones

ARTIST
gene ha

COLORIST
gloria vasquez

SEPARATOR
digital chameleon

LETTERER
willie schubert

BATMAN CREATED BY
bob kane

dc comics JENETTE KAHN PRESIDENT & EDITOR-IN-CHIEF • PAUL LEVITZ EXECUTIVE VICE PRESIDENT & PUBLISHER MIKE CARLIN EXECUTIVE EDITOR • ARCHIE GOODWIN AND JORDAN B. GORFINKEL EDITORS GEORG BREWER DESIGN DIRECTOR • AMIE BROCKWAY ART DIRECTOR • RICHARD BRUNING VP-CREATIVE DIRECTOR • PATRICK CALDON VP-FINANCE & OPERATIONS • DOROTHY CROUCH VP-LICENSED PUBLISHING TERRI CUNNINGHAM VP-MANAGING EDITOR • JOEL EHRLICH SENIOR VP-ADVERTISING & PROMOTIONS ALISON GILL EXECUTIVE DIRECTOR-MANUFACTURING • LILLIAN LASERSON VP & GENERAL COUNSEL JIM LEE EDITORIAL DIRECTOR-WILDSTORM • JOHN NEE VP & GENERAL MANAGER-WILDSTORM BOB WAYNE VP-DIRECT SALES

batman: fortunate son PUBLISHED BY DC COMICS, 1700 BROADWAY, NEW YORK, NY 10019. COPYRIGHT © 1999 DC COMICS. ALL RIGHTS RESERVED. ALL CHARACTERS FEATURED IN THIS ISSUE, THE DISTINCTIVE LIKE-NESSES THEREOF, AND ALL RELATED INDICIA ARE TRADEMARKS OF DC COMICS. THE STORIES, CHARACTERS AND INCIDENTS MENTIONED IN THIS MAGAZINE ARE ENTIRELY FICTIONAL. PRINTED ON RECYCLABLE PAPER. PRINTED IN CANADA.
DC COMICS, A DIVISION OF WARNER BROS.— A TIME WARNER ENTERTAINMENT COMPANY

COVER ART: GENE HA
ADDITIONAL COLOR AND SEPARATIONS (COVERS AND PP 4–96): MATT HOLLINGSWORTH

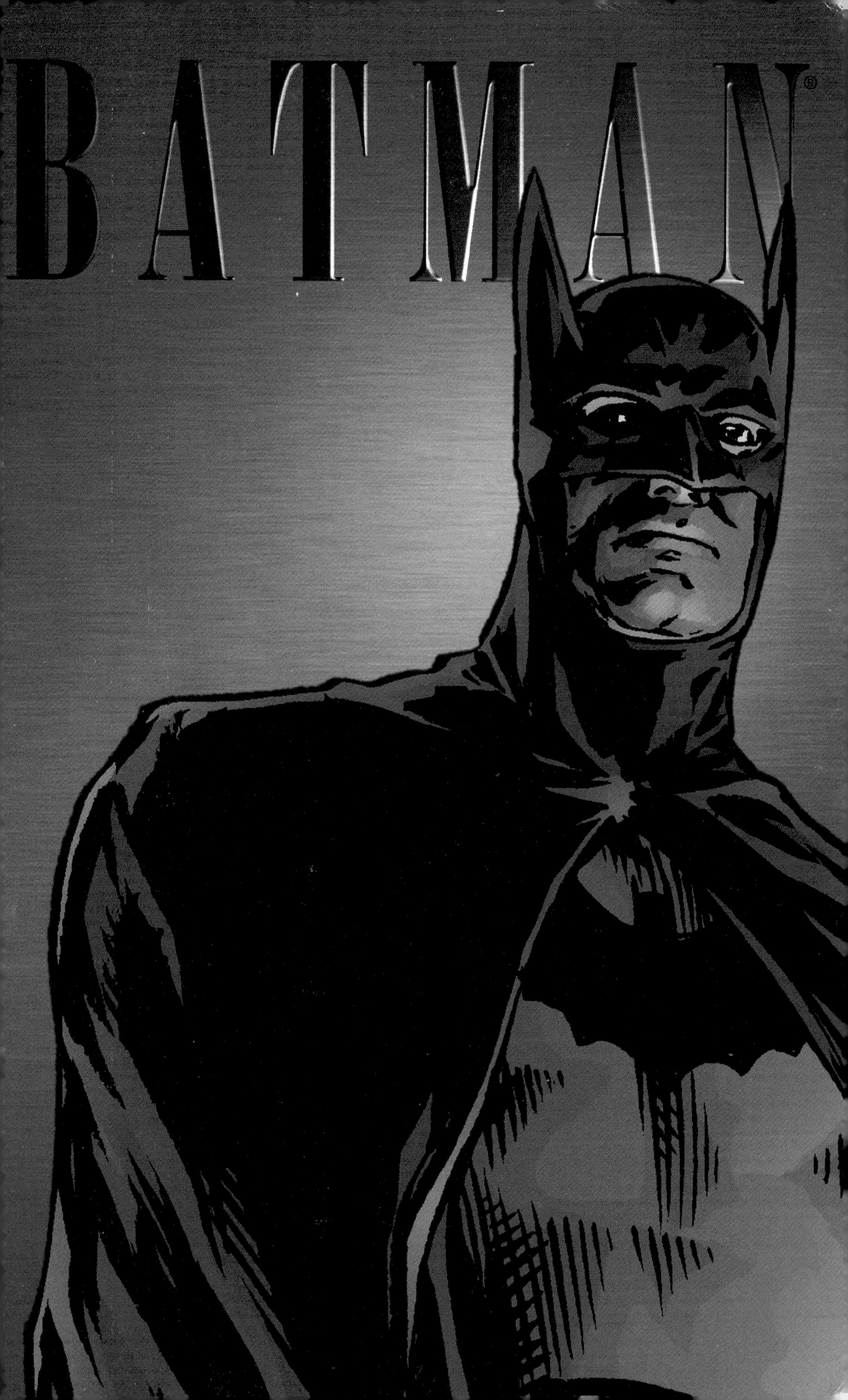
BATMAN®

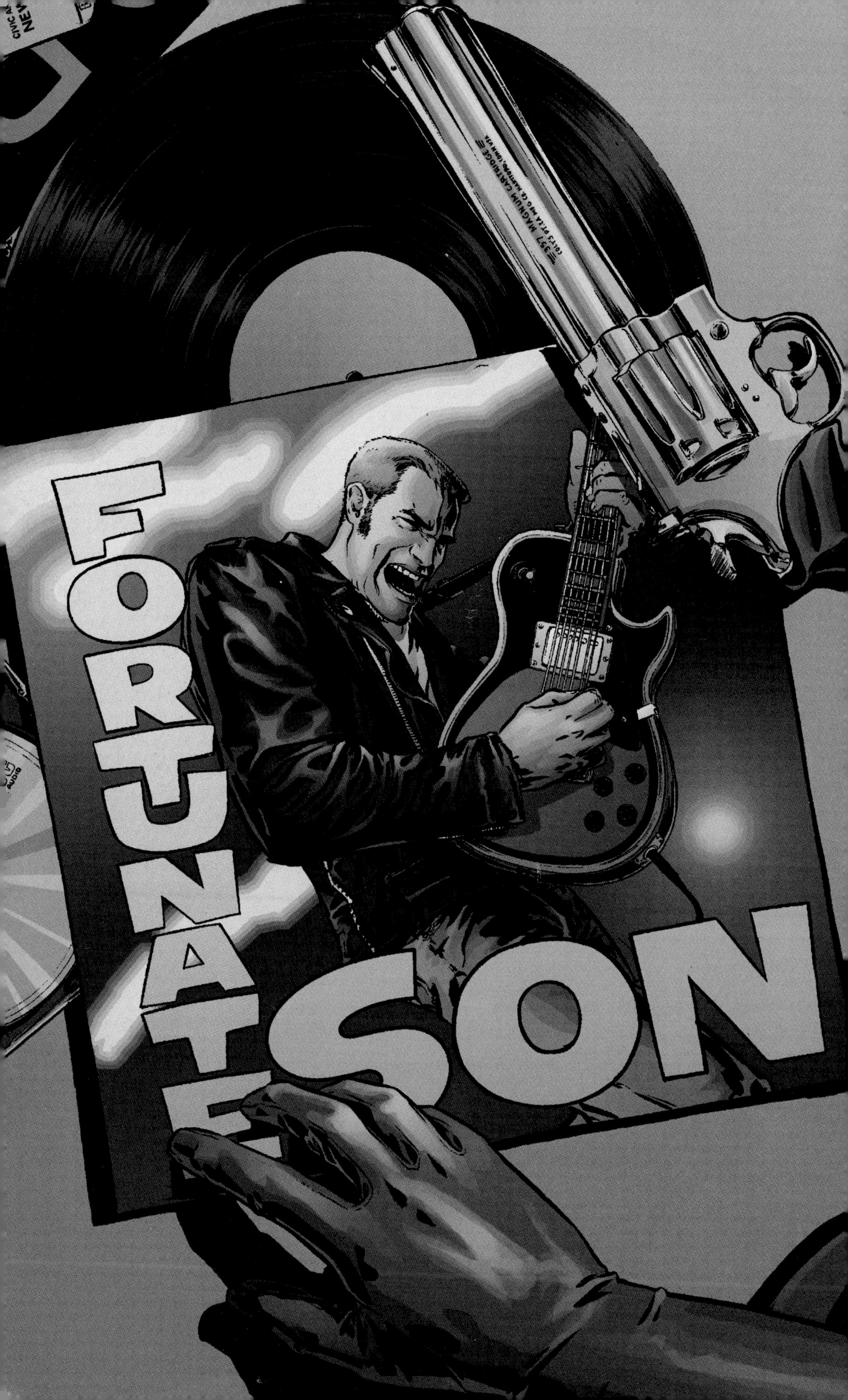
FORTUNATE SON

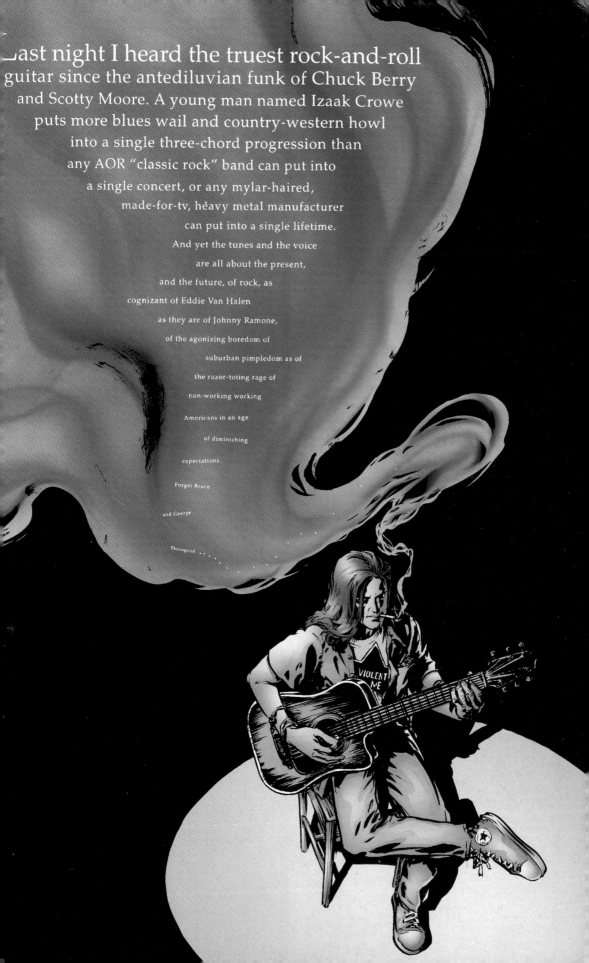

Last night I heard the truest rock-and-roll guitar since the antediluvian funk of Chuck Berry and Scotty Moore. A young man named Izaak Crowe puts more blues wail and country-western howl into a single three-chord progression than any AOR "classic rock" band can put into a single concert, or any mylar-haired, made-for-tv, heavy metal manufacturer can put into a single lifetime. And yet the tunes and the voice are all about the present, and the future, of rock, as cognizant of Eddie Van Halen as they are of Johnny Ramone, of the agonizing boredom of suburban pimpledom as of the razor-toting rage of non-working working Americans in an age of diminishing expectations.

Forget Bruce and George Thorogood . . .

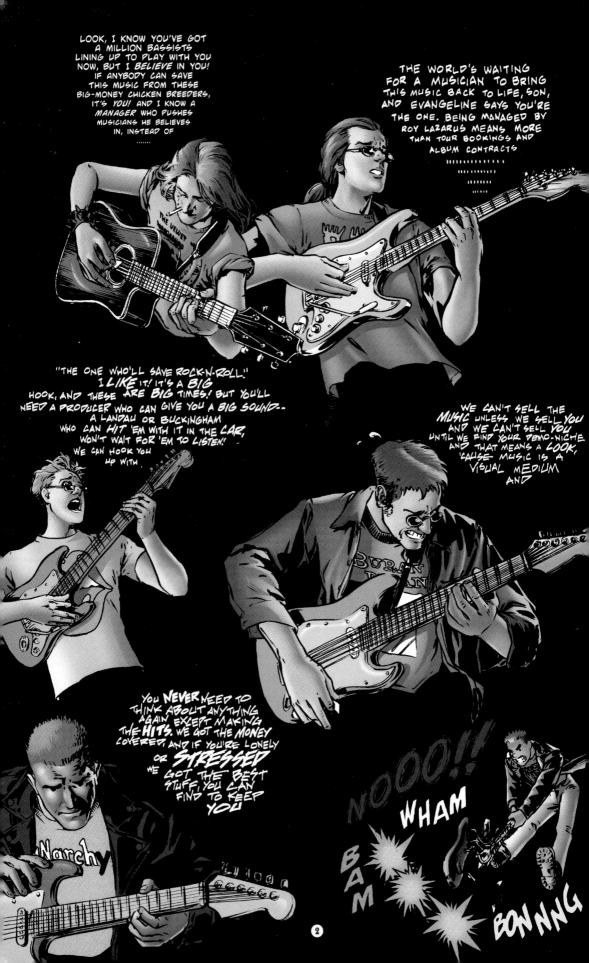

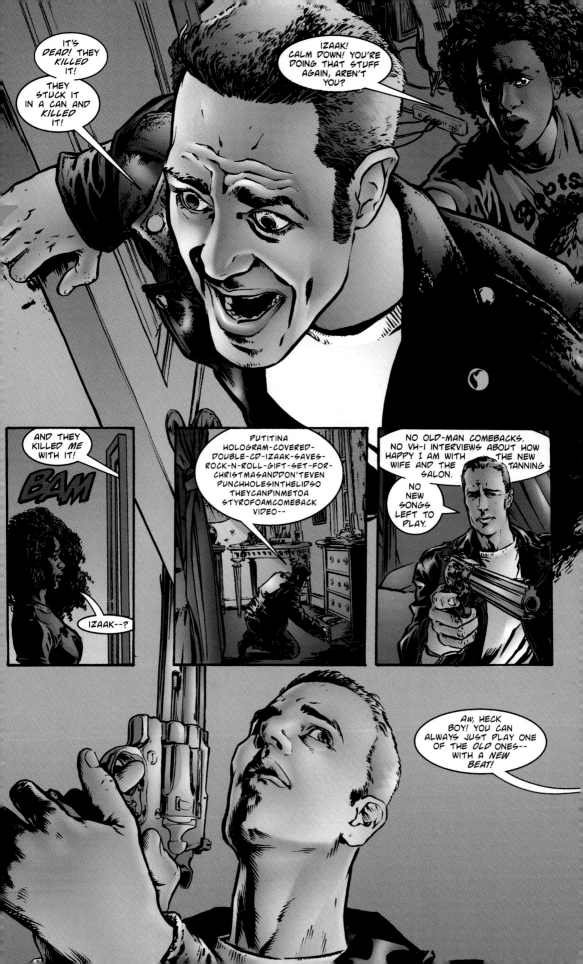

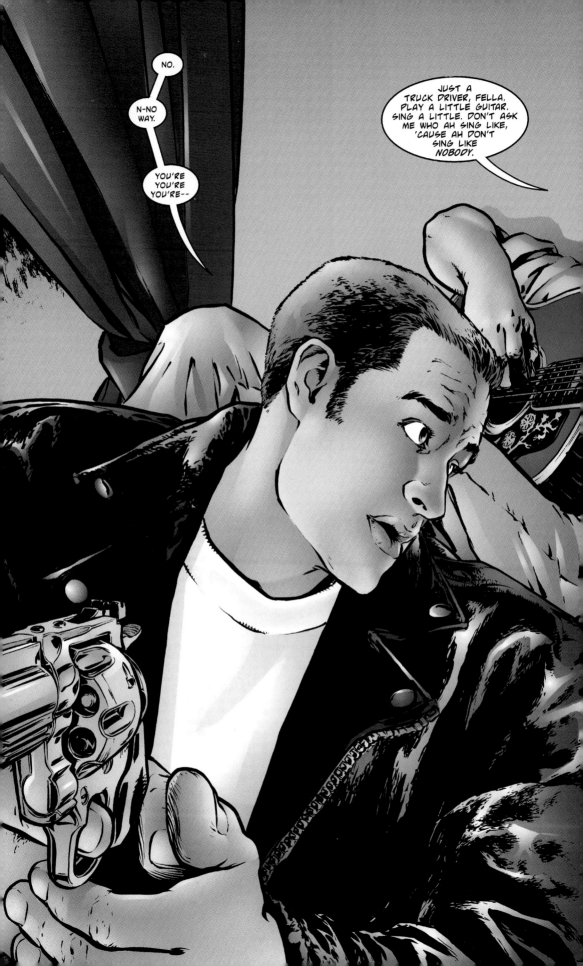

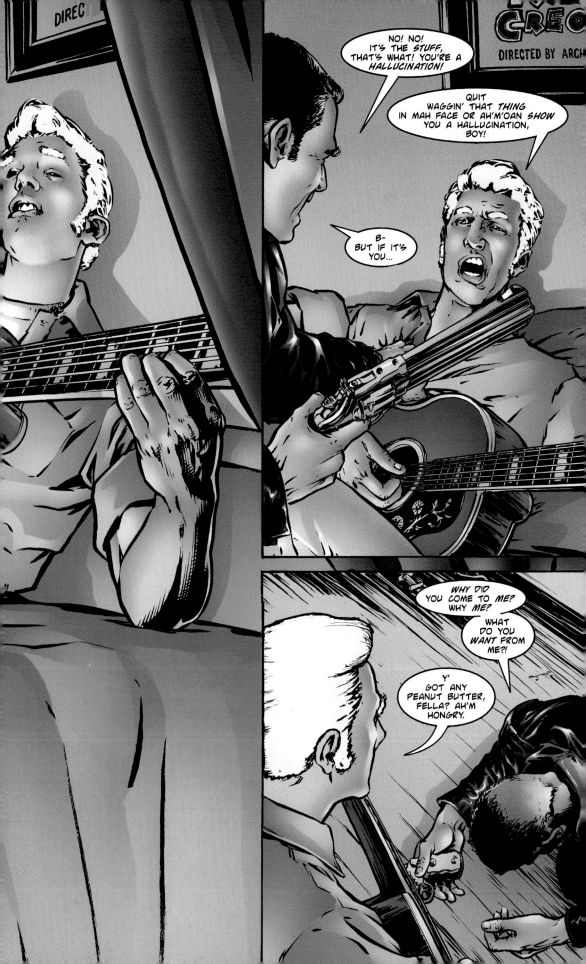

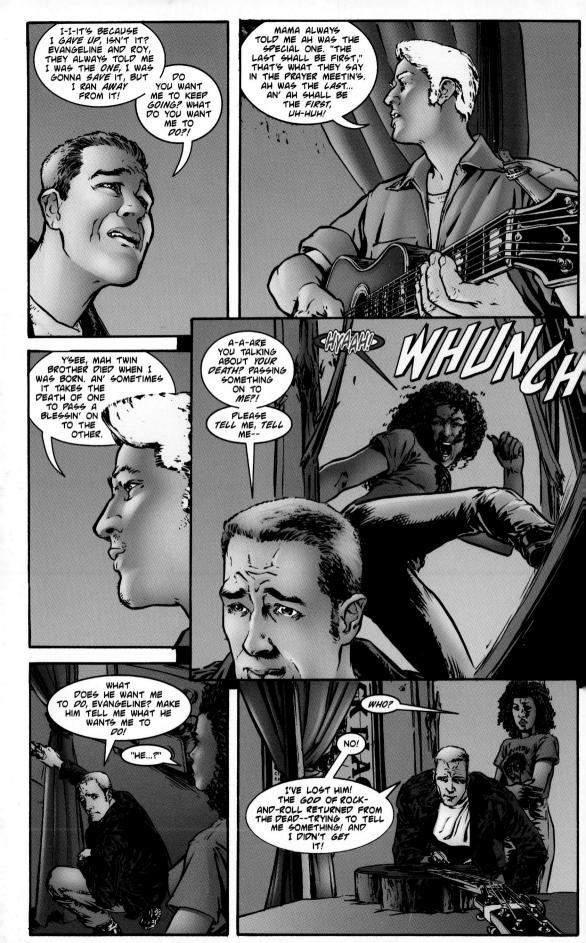

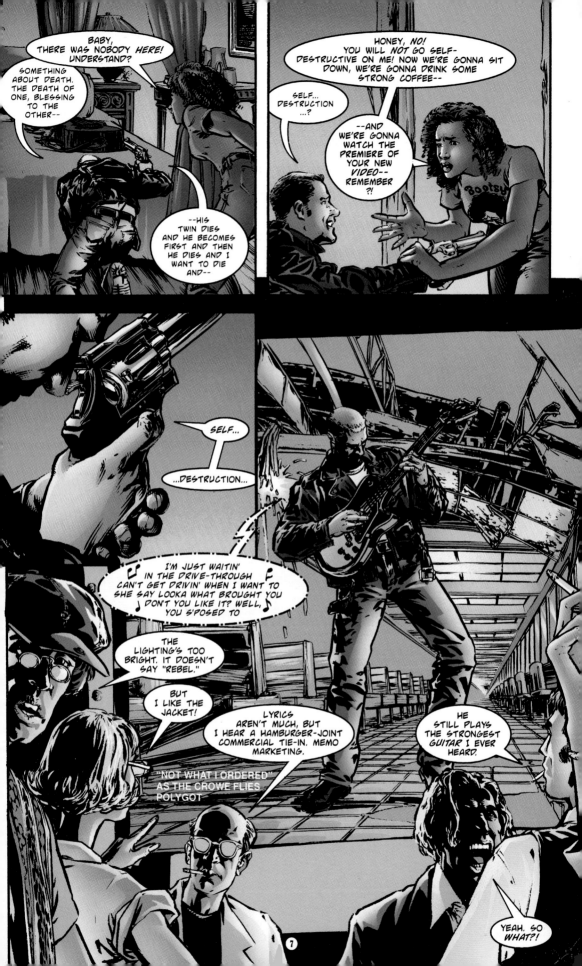

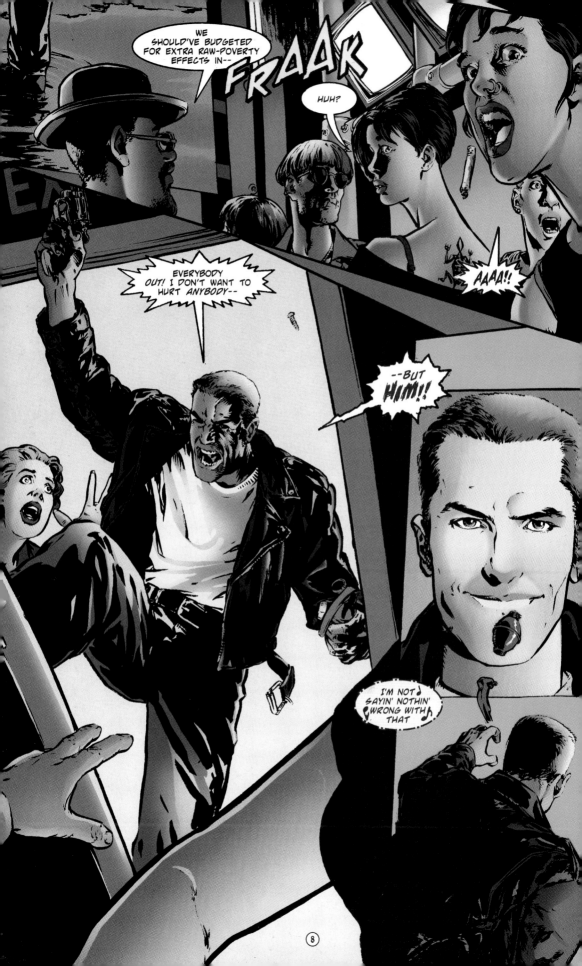

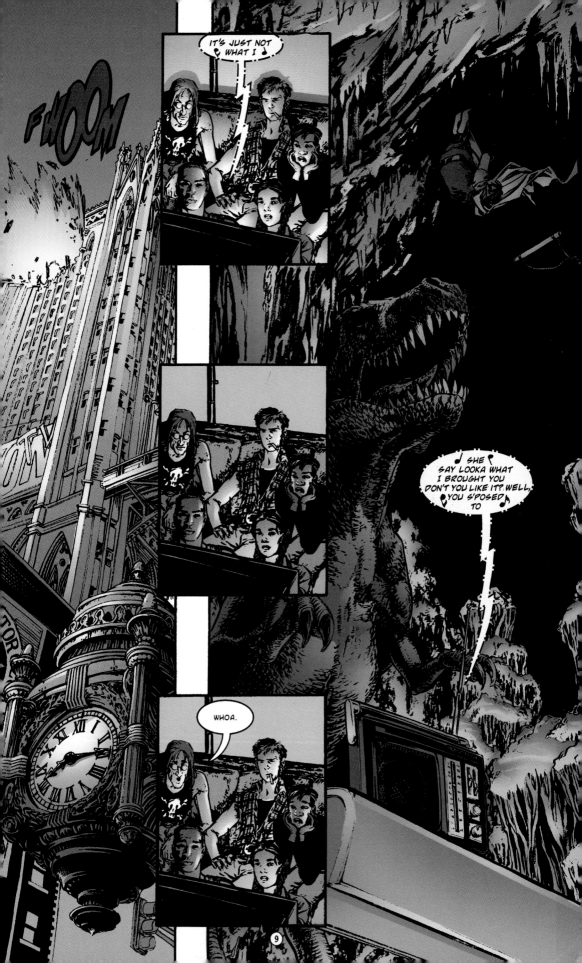

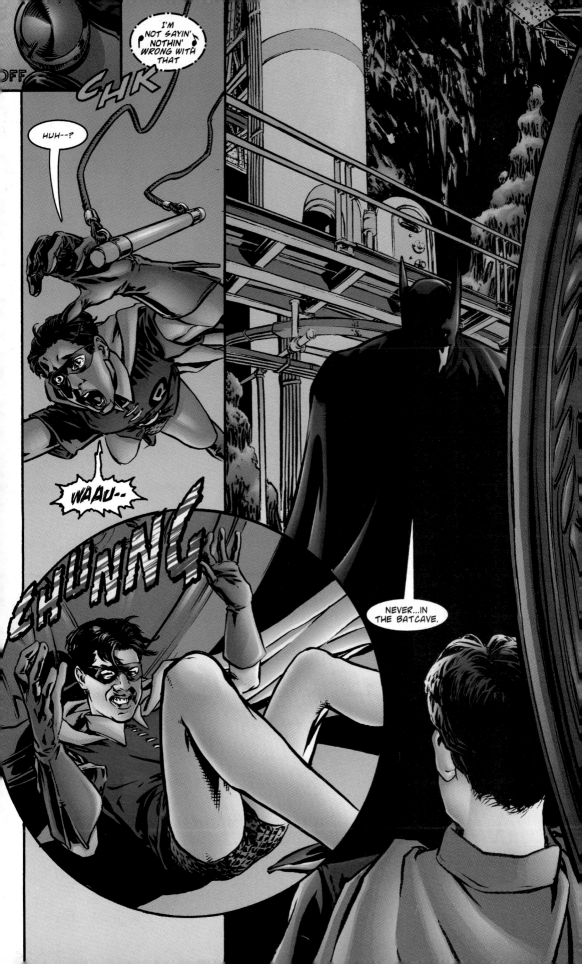

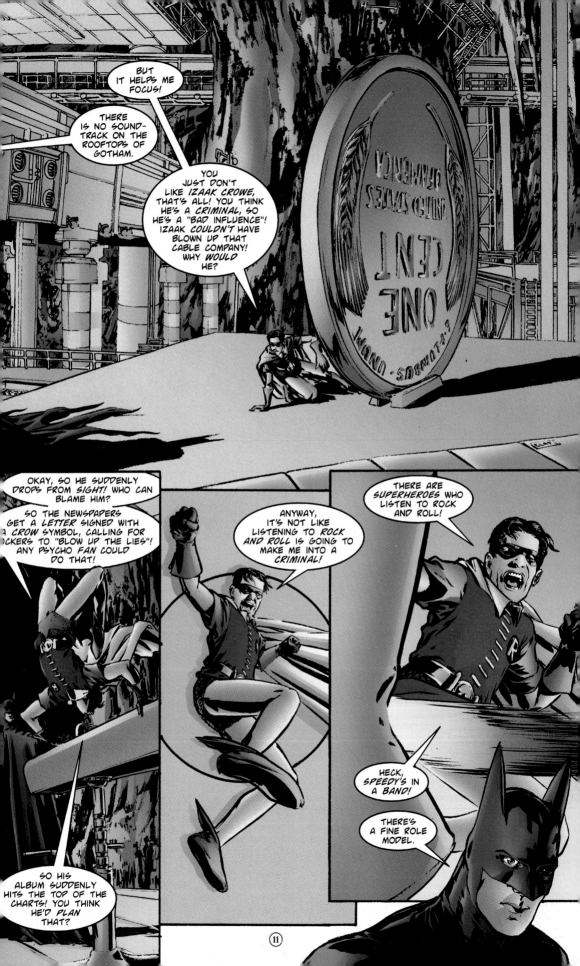

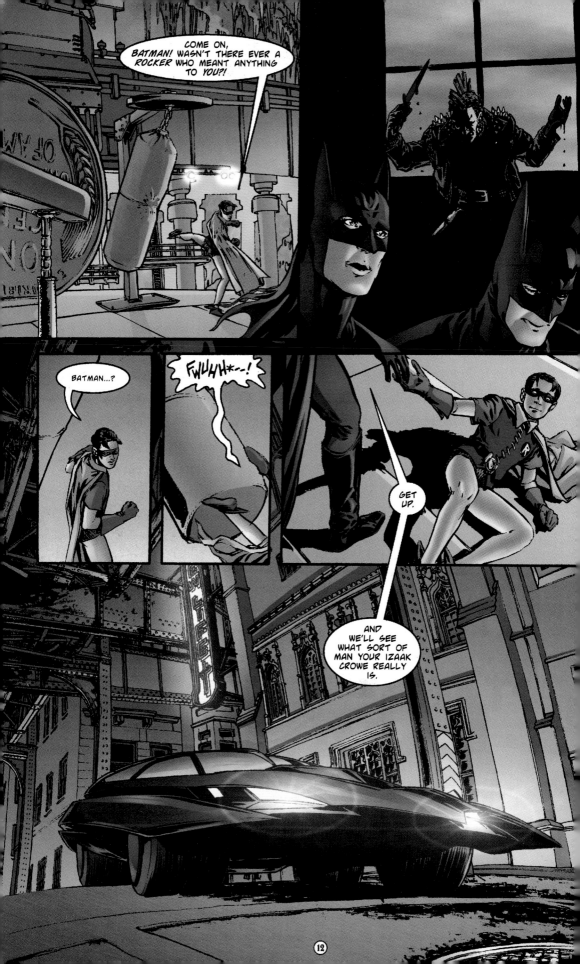

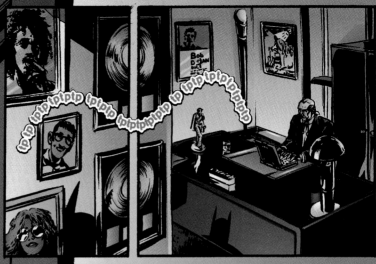

tptp tptp tptp tptp tp tptptptptp tp tptptptptptp

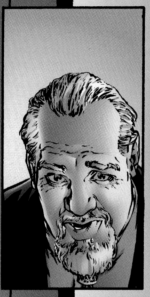

R O Y
LAZARUS
✝
♛
T A L E N T
MANAGEMENT

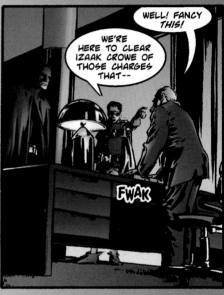

WELL! FANCY THIS!

WE'RE HERE TO CLEAR IZAAK CROWE OF THOSE CHARGES THAT--

FWAK

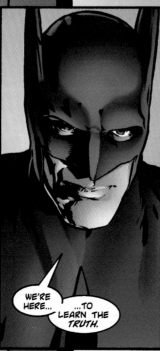

WE'RE HERE... ...TO LEARN THE TRUTH.

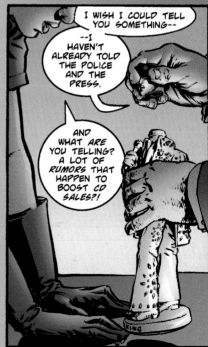

I WISH I COULD TELL YOU SOMETHING-- --I HAVEN'T ALREADY TOLD THE POLICE AND THE PRESS.

AND WHAT ARE YOU TELLING? A LOT OF RUMORS THAT HAPPEN TO BOOST CD SALES?!

KING

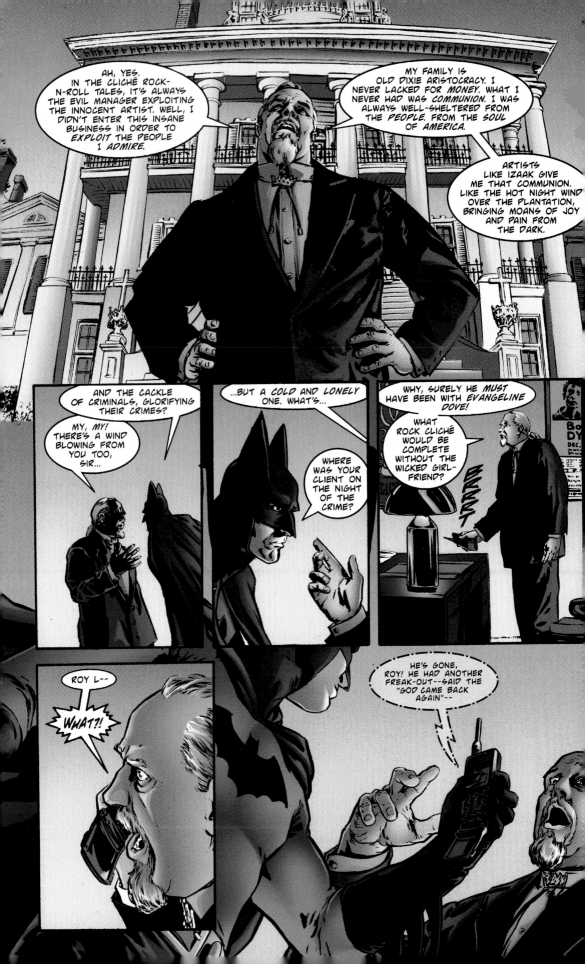

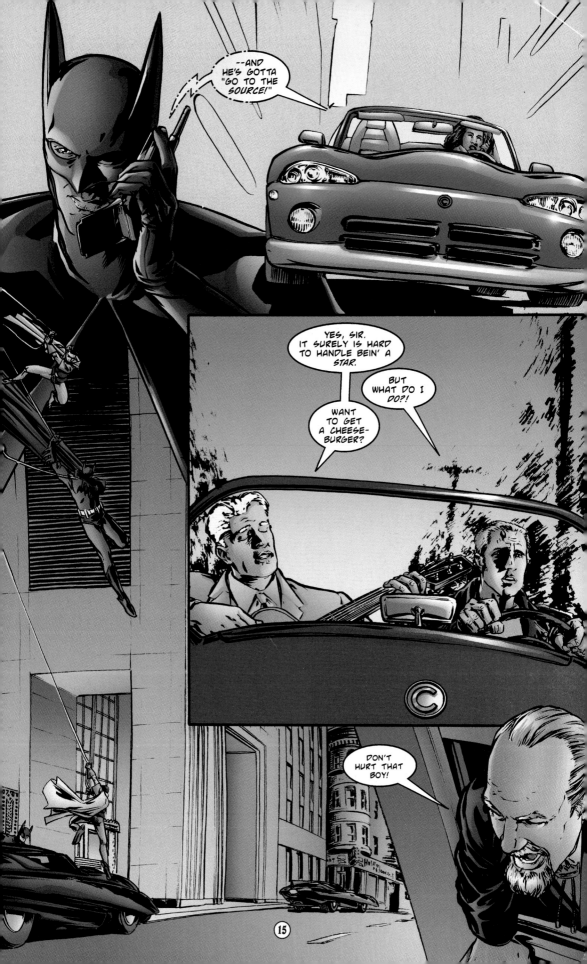

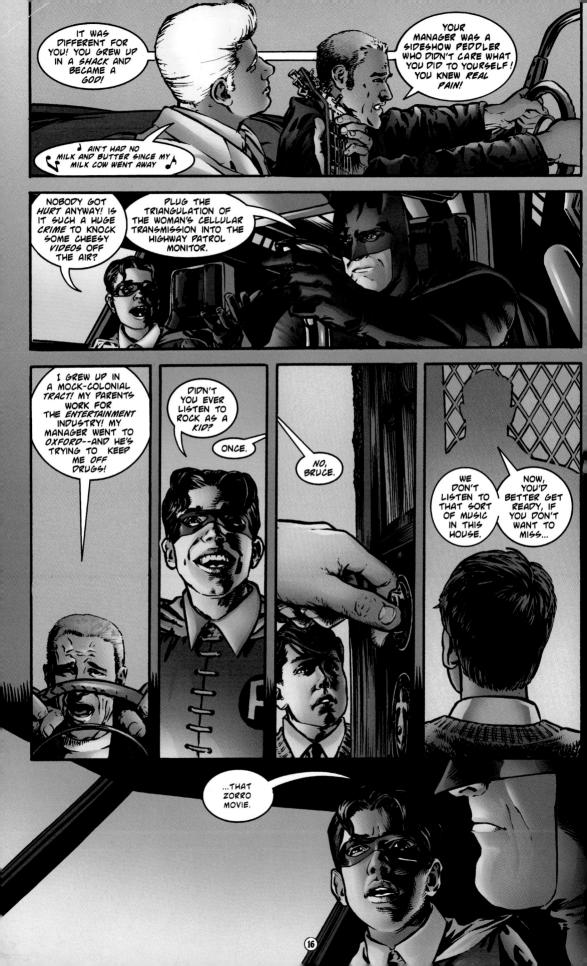

IT WAS DIFFERENT FOR YOU! YOU GREW UP IN A SHACK AND BECAME A GOD!

YOUR MANAGER WAS A SIDESHOW PEDDLER WHO DIDN'T CARE WHAT YOU DID TO YOURSELF! YOU KNEW REAL PAIN!

♪ AIN'T HAD NO MILK AND BUTTER SINCE MY MILK COW WENT AWAY ♪

NOBODY GOT HURT ANYWAY! IS IT SUCH A HUGE CRIME TO KNOCK SOME CHEESY VIDEOS OFF THE AIR?

PLUG THE TRIANGULATION OF THE WOMAN'S CELLULAR TRANSMISSION INTO THE HIGHWAY PATROL MONITOR.

I GREW UP IN A MOCK-COLONIAL TRACT! MY PARENTS WORK FOR THE ENTERTAINMENT INDUSTRY! MY MANAGER WENT TO OXFORD--AND HE'S TRYING TO KEEP ME OFF DRUGS!

DIDN'T YOU EVER LISTEN TO ROCK AS A KID?

ONCE.

NO, BRUCE.

WE DON'T LISTEN TO THAT SORT OF MUSIC IN THIS HOUSE.

NOW, YOU'D BETTER GET READY, IF YOU DON'T WANT TO MISS...

...THAT ZORRO MOVIE.

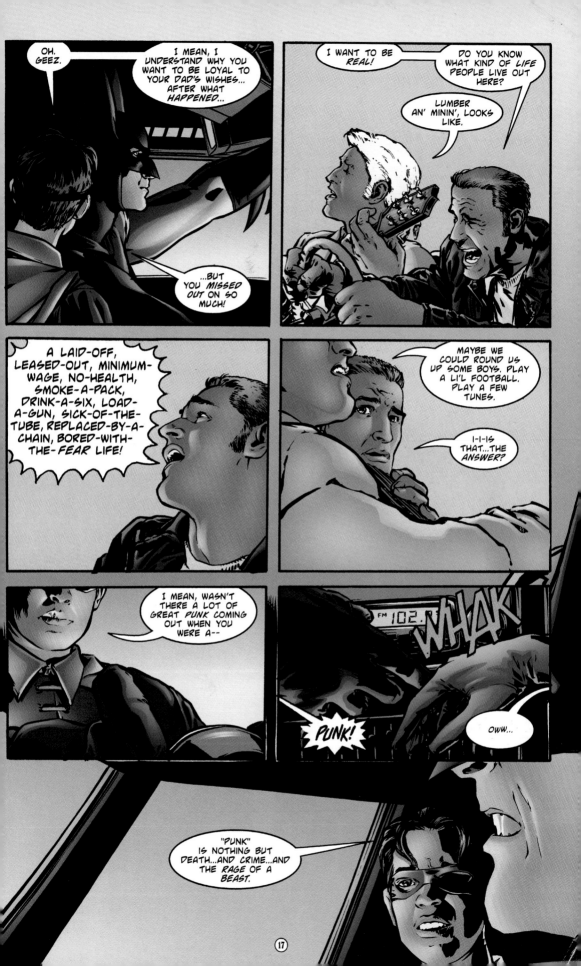

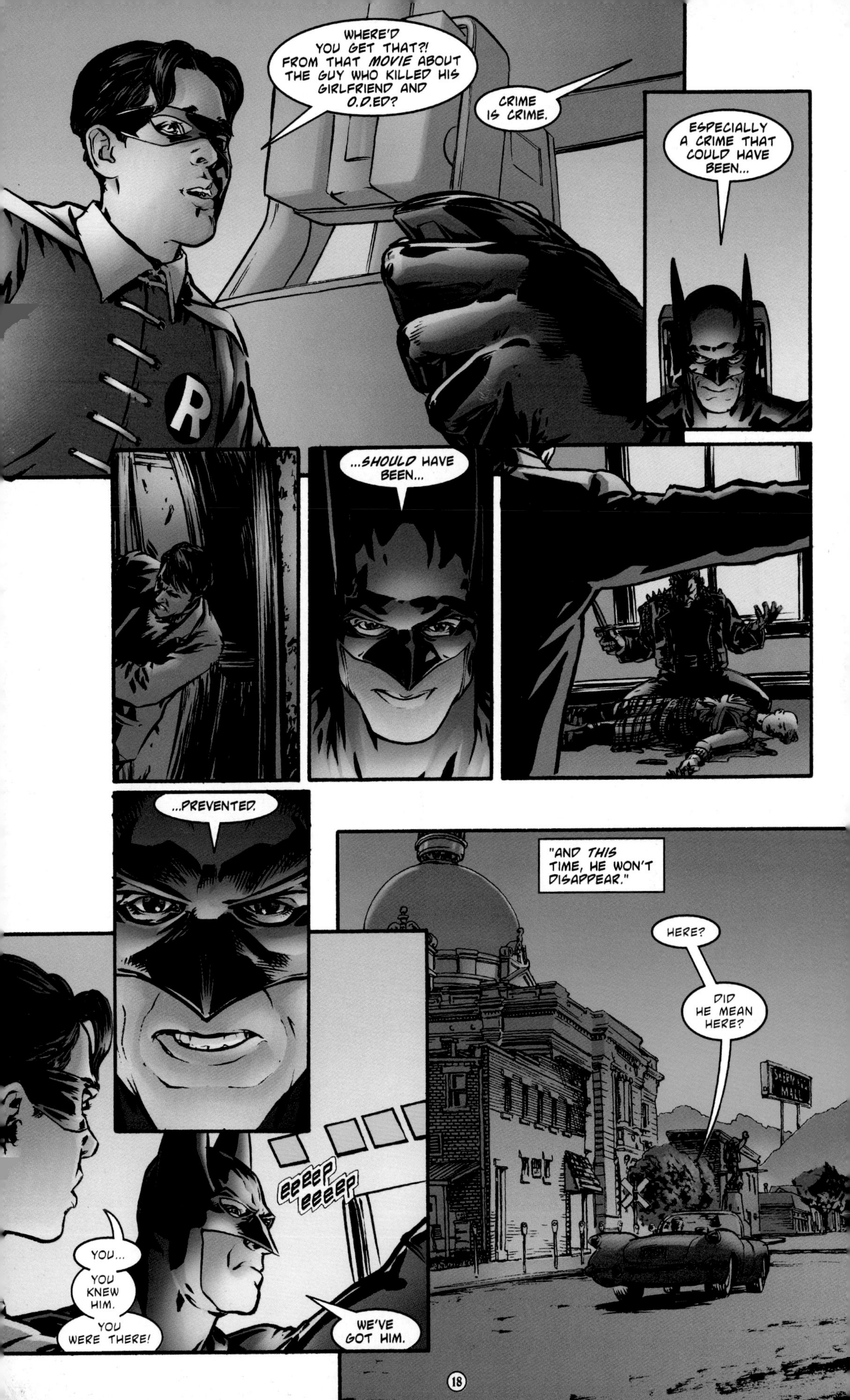

WHERE'D YOU GET THAT?! FROM THAT MOVIE ABOUT THE GUY WHO KILLED HIS GIRLFRIEND AND O.D.ED?
CRIME IS CRIME.
ESPECIALLY A CRIME THAT COULD HAVE BEEN...
...SHOULD HAVE BEEN...
...PREVENTED.
"AND THIS TIME, HE WON'T DISAPPEAR."
HERE?
DID HE MEAN HERE?
EEEEP EEEEP
YOU...
YOU KNEW HIM.
YOU WERE THERE!
WE'VE GOT HIM.

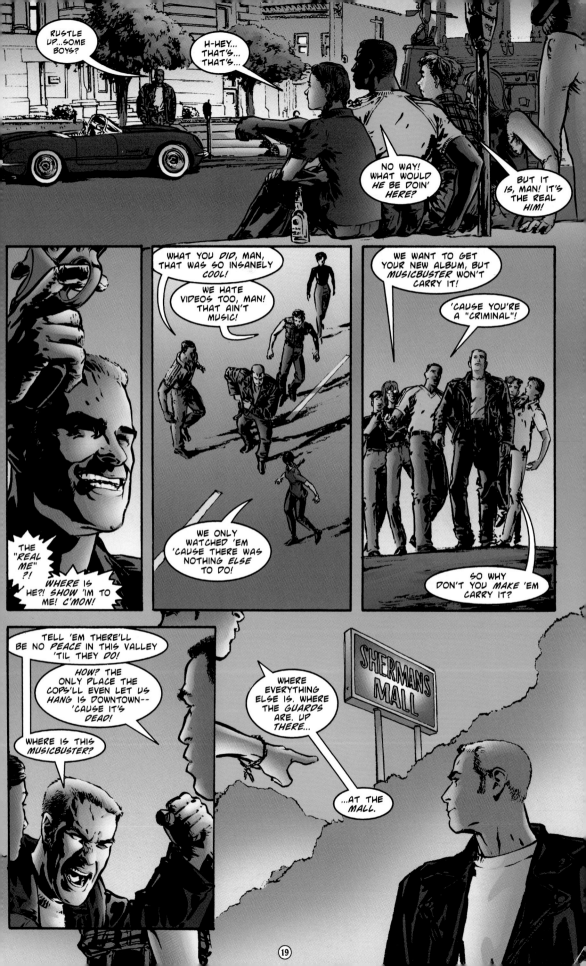

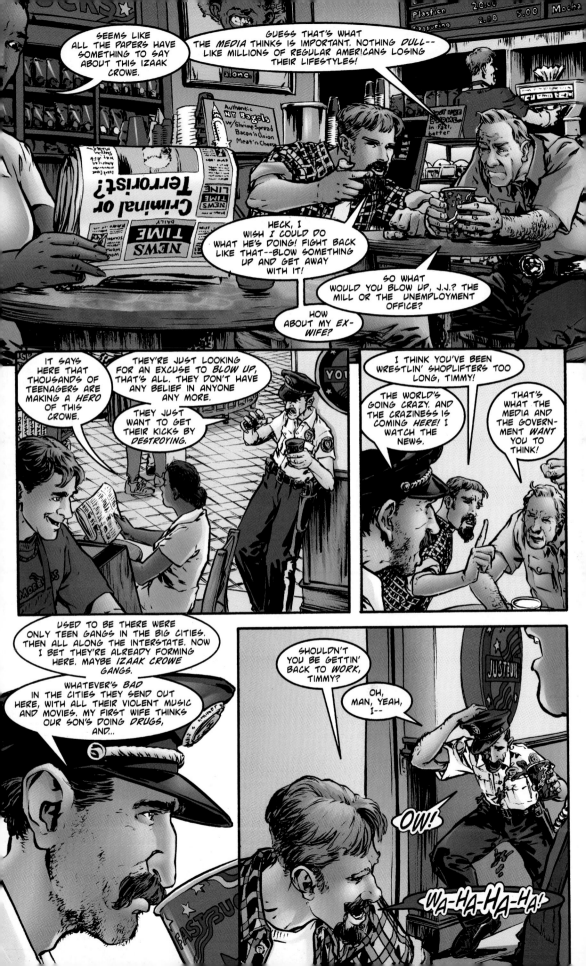

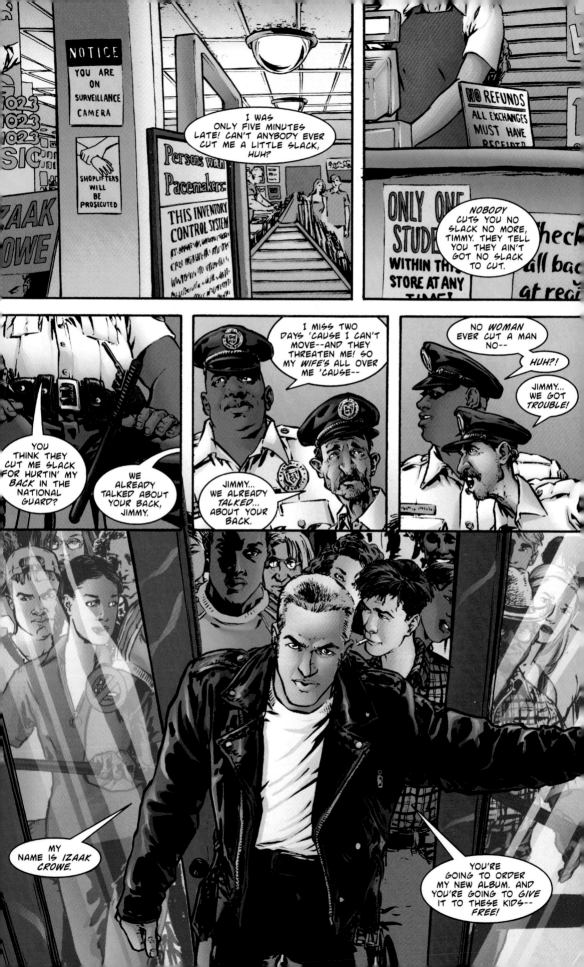

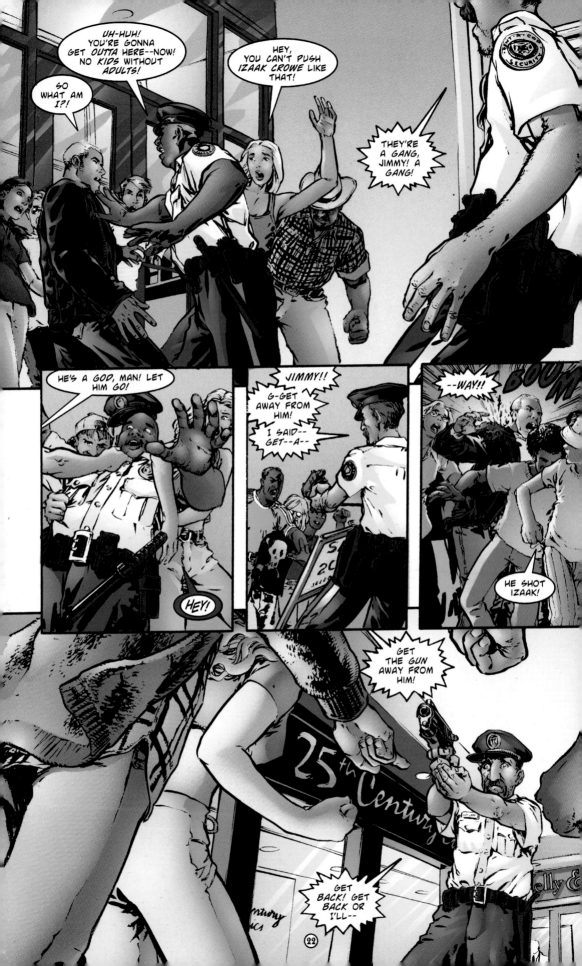

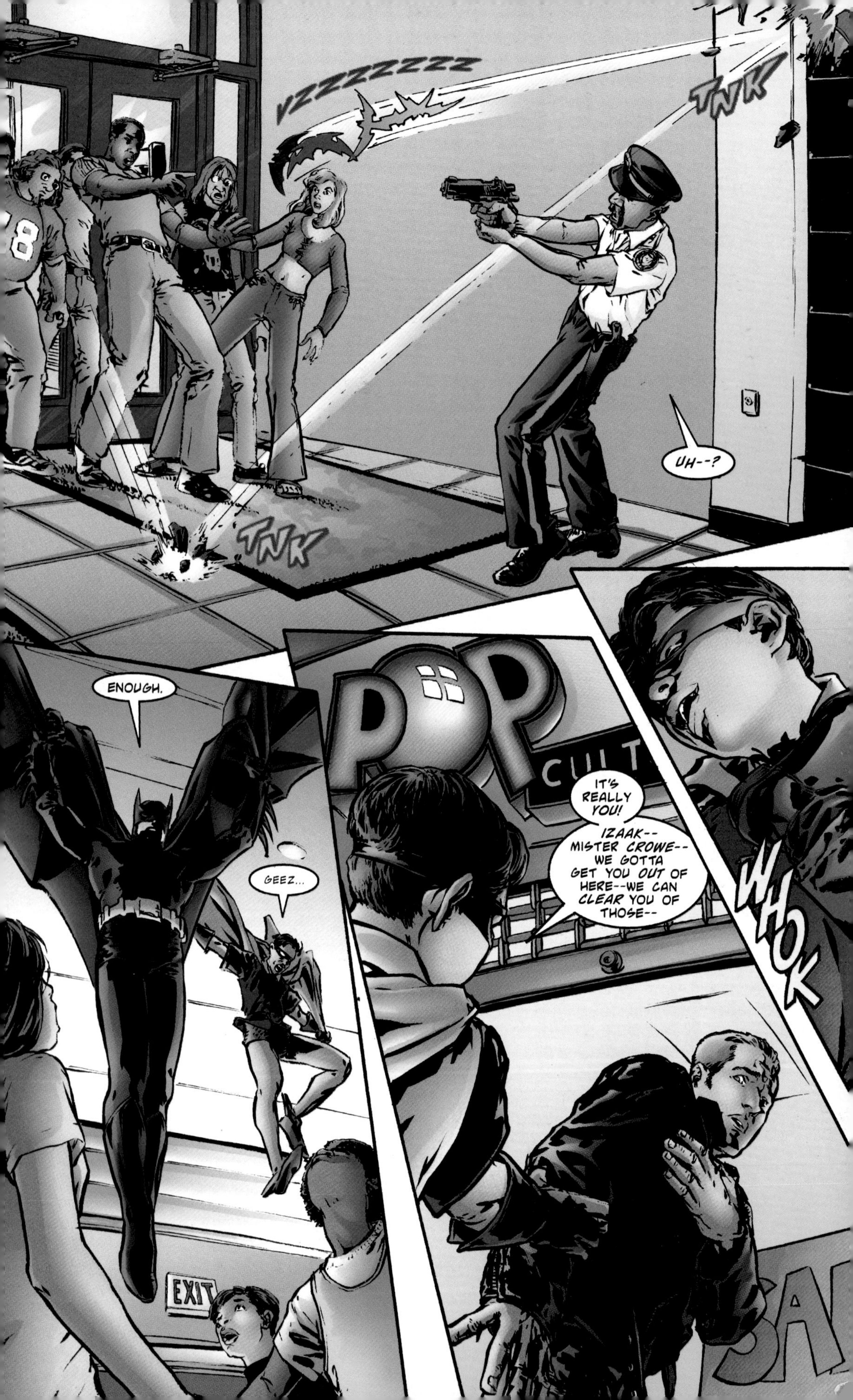
VZZZZZZZZ
TNK
UH--?
TNK
ENOUGH.
GEEZ...
POP
CULT
IT'S REALLY YOU!
IZAAK-- MISTER CROWE-- WE GOTTA GET YOU OUT OF HERE--WE CAN CLEAR YOU OF THOSE--
WHOK
EXIT

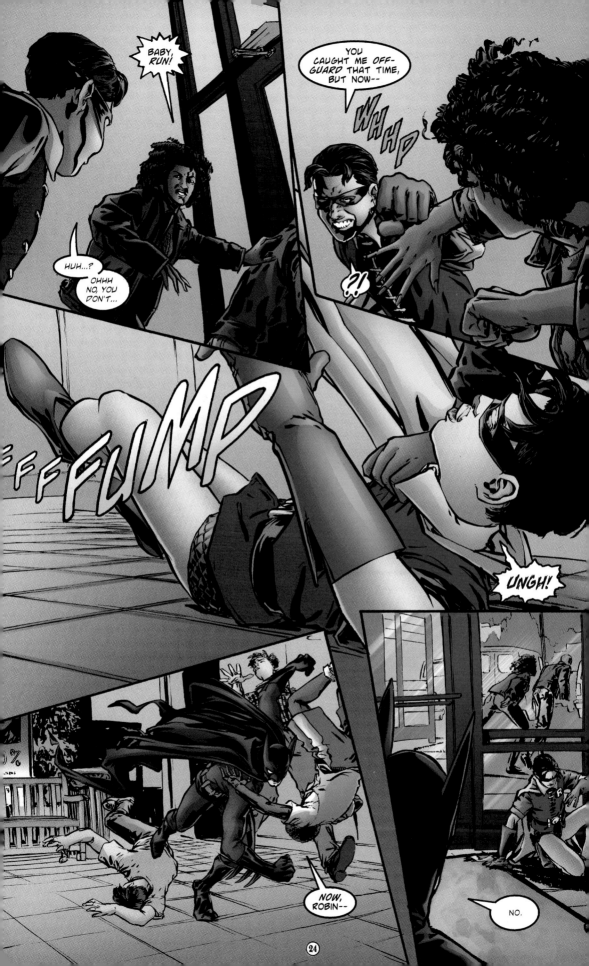

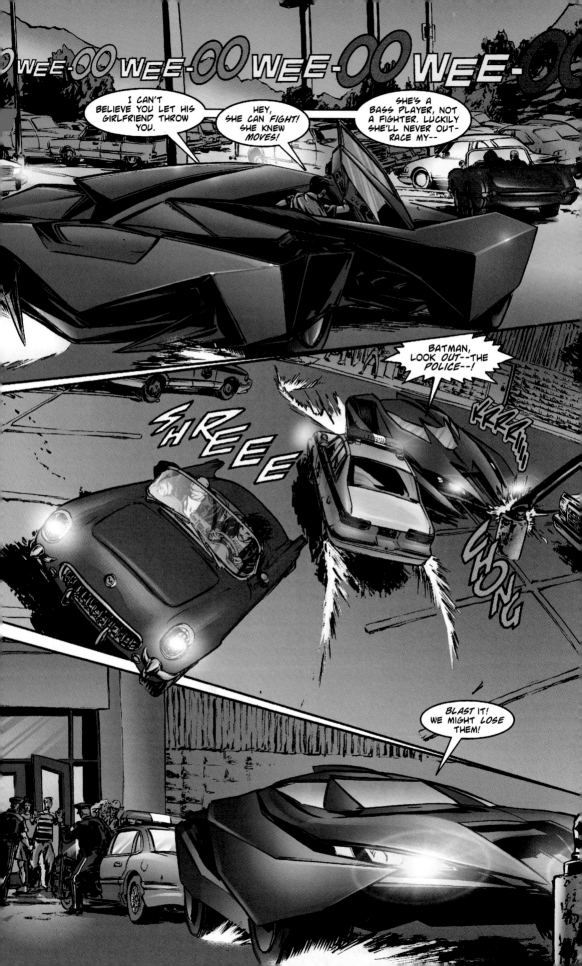

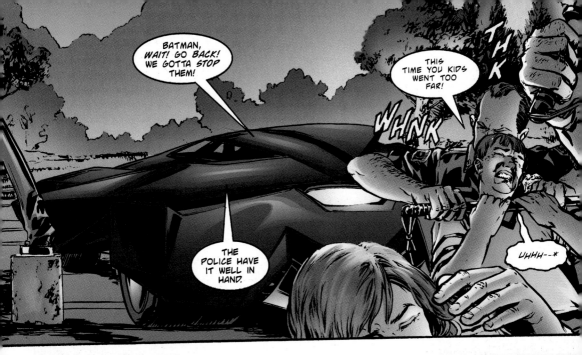

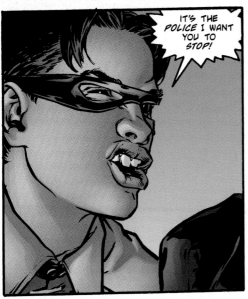

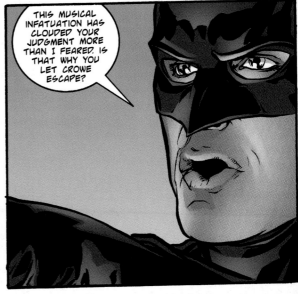

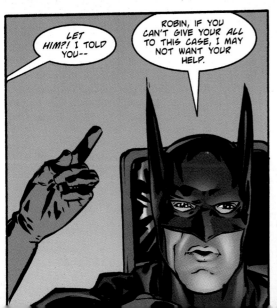

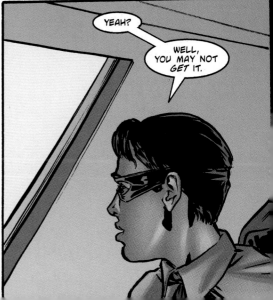

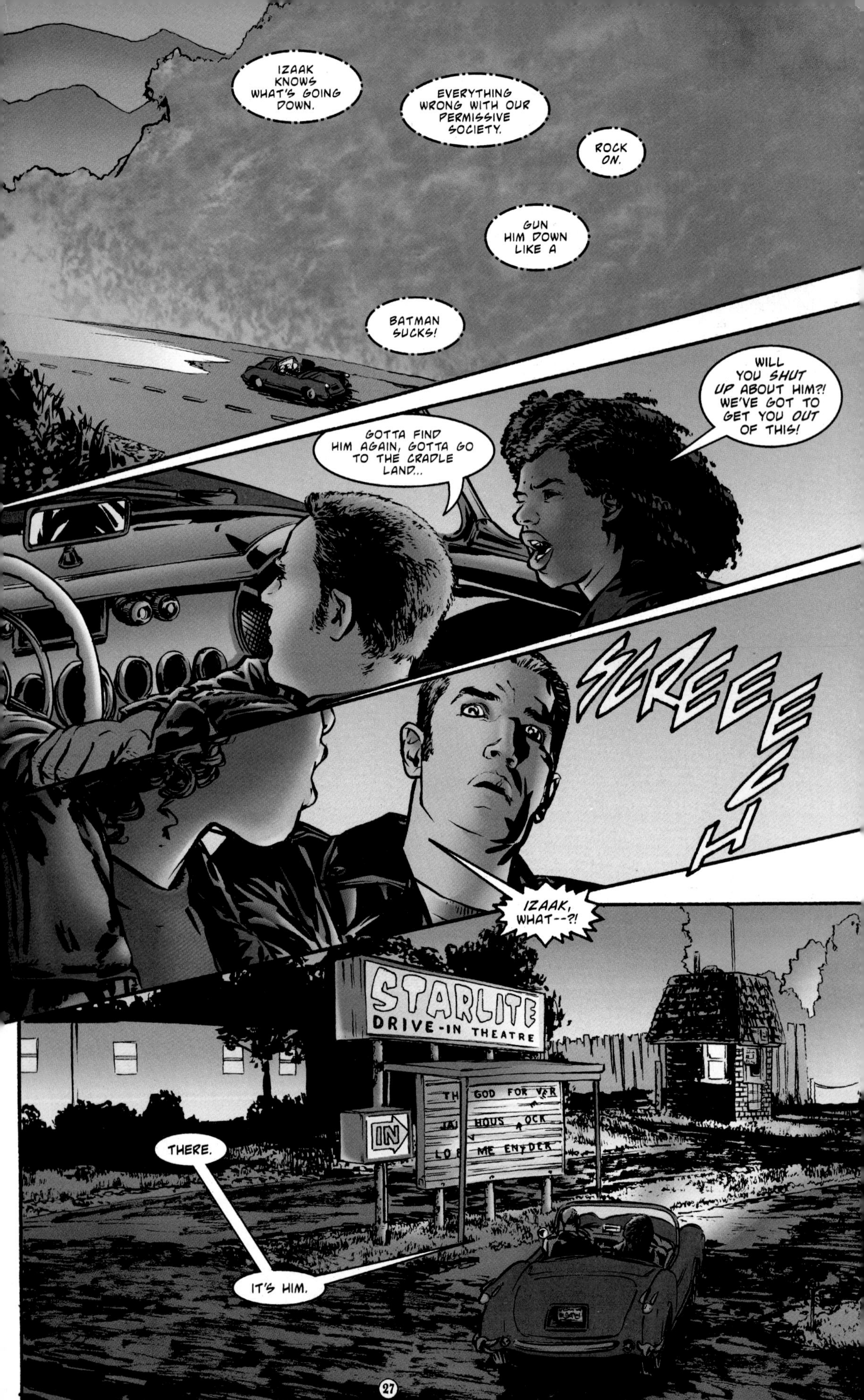
IZAAK KNOWS WHAT'S GOING DOWN.
EVERYTHING WRONG WITH OUR PERMISSIVE SOCIETY.
ROCK ON.
GUN HIM DOWN LIKE A
BATMAN SUCKS!
GOTTA FIND HIM AGAIN, GOTTA GO TO THE CRADLE LAND...
WILL YOU SHUT UP ABOUT HIM?! WE'VE GOT TO GET YOU OUT OF THIS!
SCREEECH
IZAAK, WHAT--?!
STARLITE
DRIVE-IN THEATRE
TH GOD FOR VER
JA HOUS OCK
LO ME EN DER
IN
THERE.
IT'S HIM.

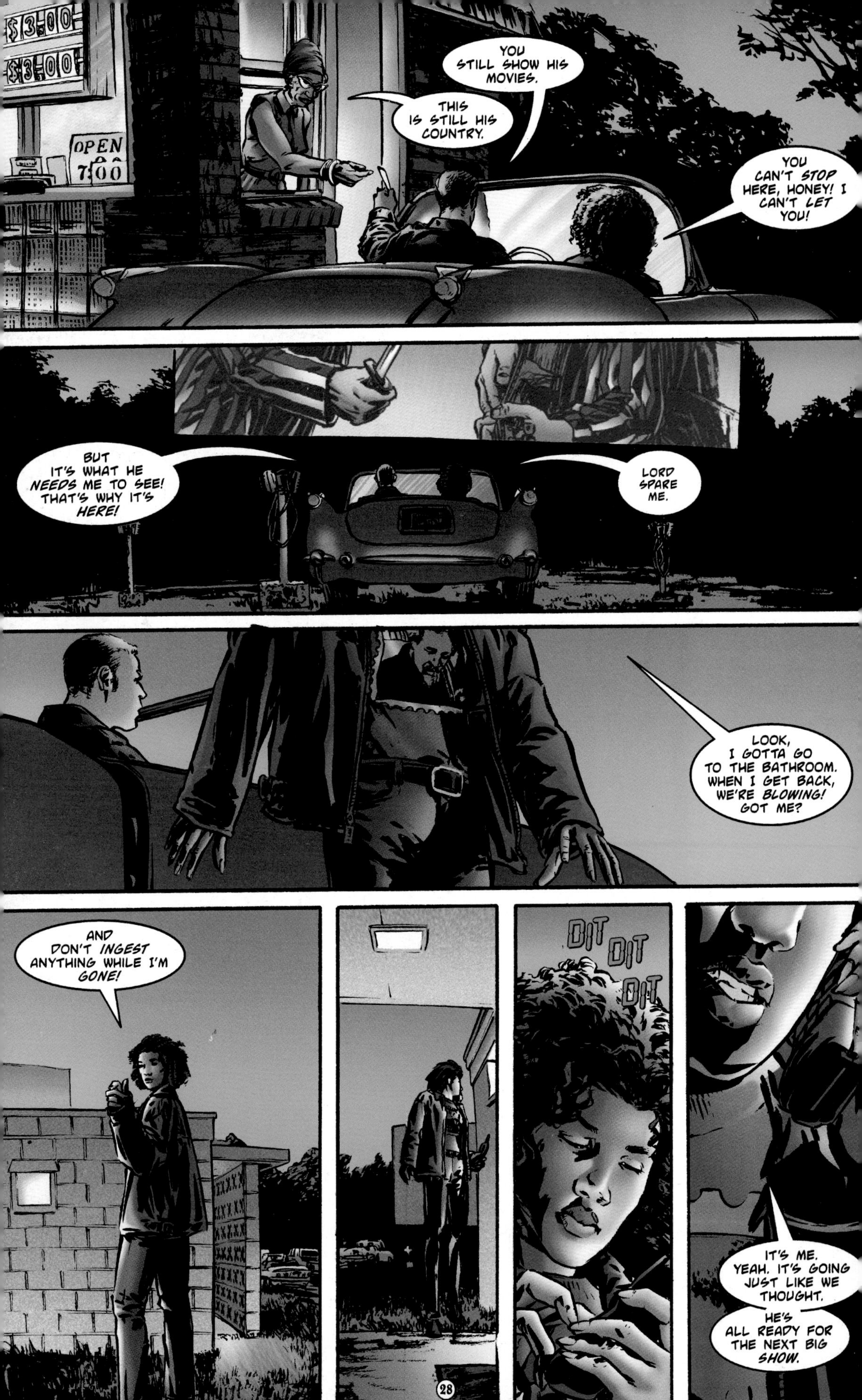
$3.00
$3.00
OPEN
7:00
YOU STILL SHOW HIS MOVIES.
THIS IS STILL HIS COUNTRY.
YOU CAN'T *STOP* HERE, HONEY! I CAN'T *LET* YOU!
BUT IT'S WHAT HE *NEEDS* ME TO SEE! THAT'S WHY IT'S *HERE!*
LORD SPARE ME.
LOOK, I GOTTA GO TO THE BATHROOM. WHEN I GET BACK, WE'RE *BLOWING!* GOT ME?
AND DON'T *INGEST* ANYTHING WHILE I'M *GONE!*
DIT DIT DIT
IT'S ME. YEAH. IT'S GOING JUST LIKE WE THOUGHT.
HE'S ALL READY FOR THE NEXT BIG *SHOW.*

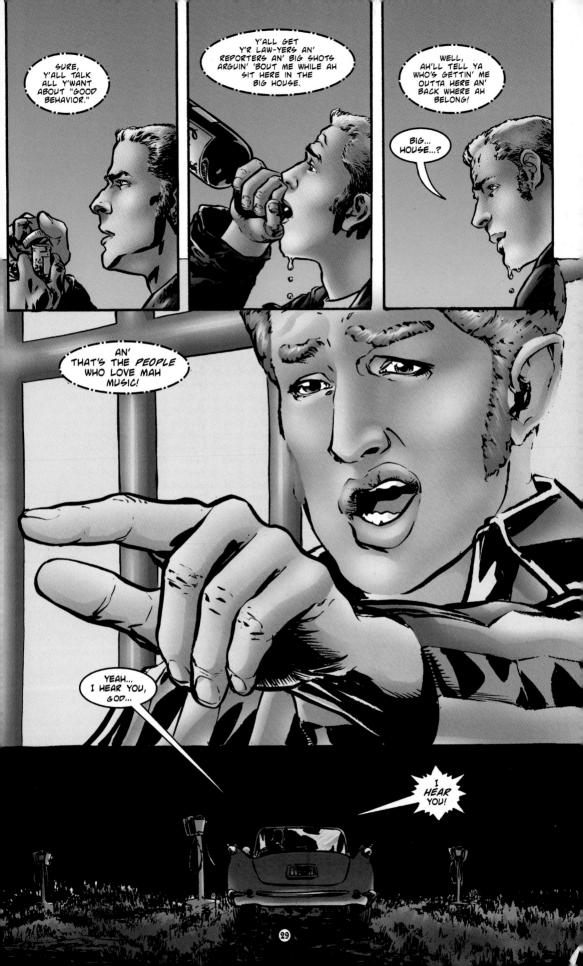

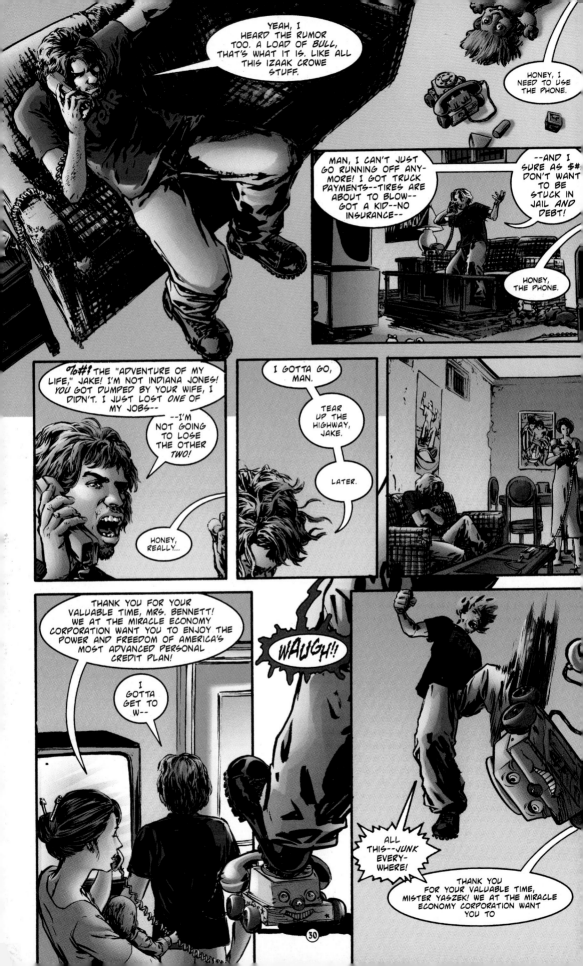

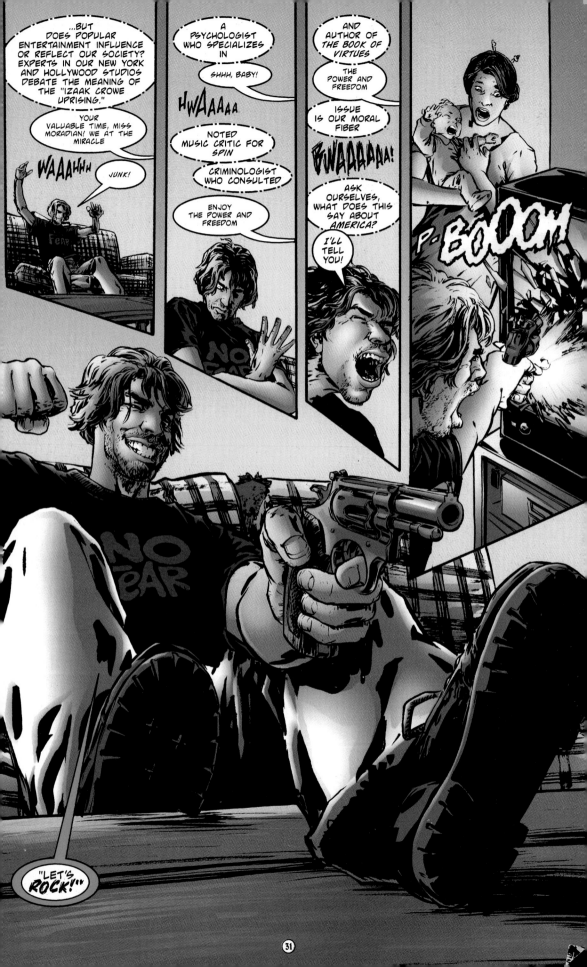

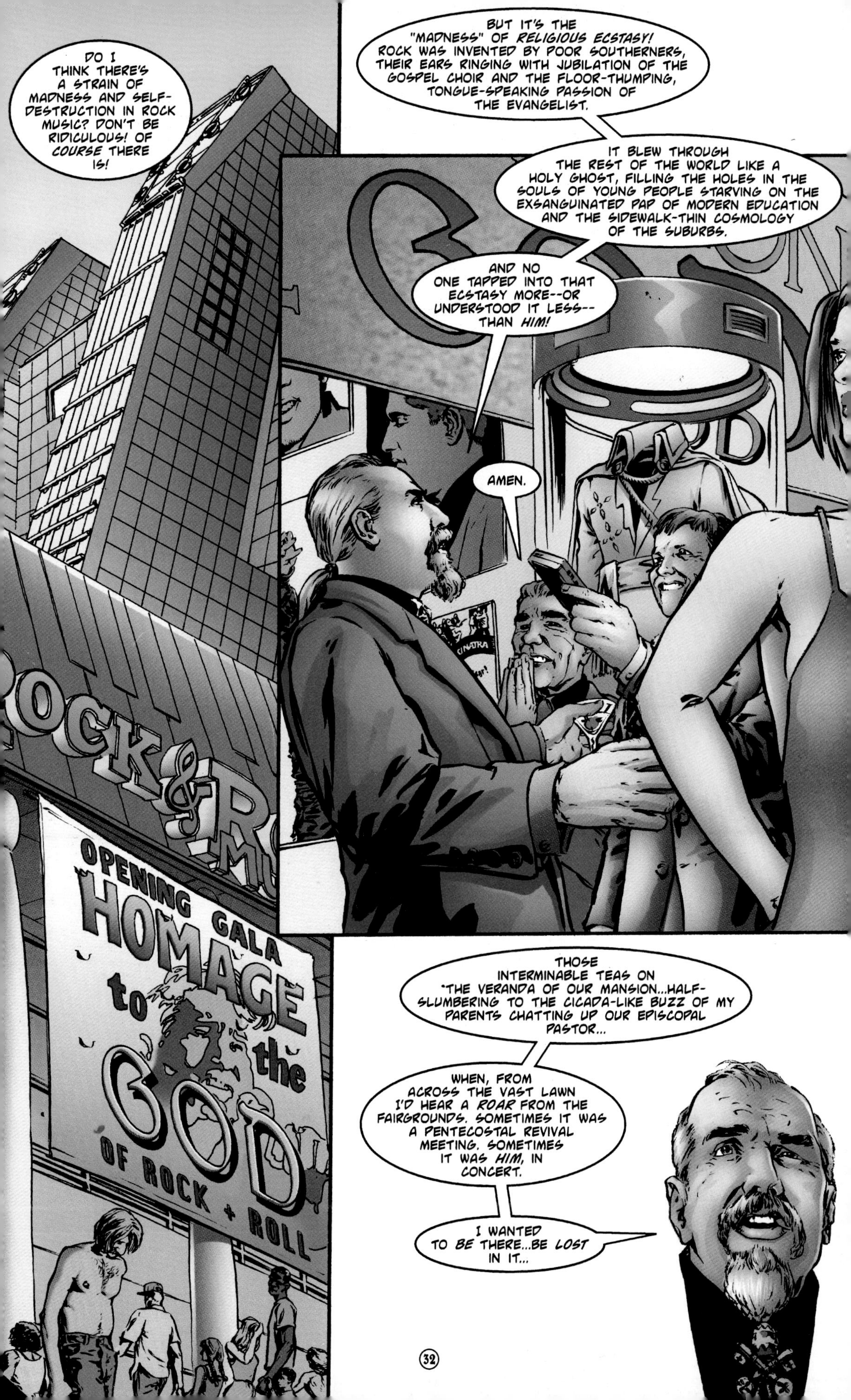
DO I THINK THERE'S A STRAIN OF MADNESS AND SELF-DESTRUCTION IN ROCK MUSIC? DON'T BE RIDICULOUS! OF COURSE THERE IS!
OPENING GALA
HOMAGE to the GOD OF ROCK + ROLL
BUT IT'S THE "MADNESS" OF *RELIGIOUS ECSTASY!* ROCK WAS INVENTED BY POOR SOUTHERNERS, THEIR EARS RINGING WITH JUBILATION OF THE GOSPEL CHOIR AND THE FLOOR-THUMPING, TONGUE-SPEAKING PASSION OF THE EVANGELIST.
IT BLEW THROUGH THE REST OF THE WORLD LIKE A HOLY GHOST, FILLING THE HOLES IN THE SOULS OF YOUNG PEOPLE STARVING ON THE EXSANGUINATED PAP OF MODERN EDUCATION AND THE SIDEWALK-THIN COSMOLOGY OF THE SUBURBS.
AND NO ONE TAPPED INTO THAT ECSTASY MORE--OR UNDERSTOOD IT LESS--THAN *HIM!*
AMEN.
THOSE INTERMINABLE TEAS ON THE VERANDA OF OUR MANSION...HALF-SLUMBERING TO THE CICADA-LIKE BUZZ OF MY PARENTS CHATTING UP OUR EPISCOPAL PASTOR...
WHEN, FROM ACROSS THE VAST LAWN I'D HEAR A *ROAR* FROM THE FAIRGROUNDS. SOMETIMES IT WAS A PENTECOSTAL REVIVAL MEETING. SOMETIMES IT WAS *HIM*, IN CONCERT.
I WANTED TO *BE* THERE...BE *LOST* IN IT...

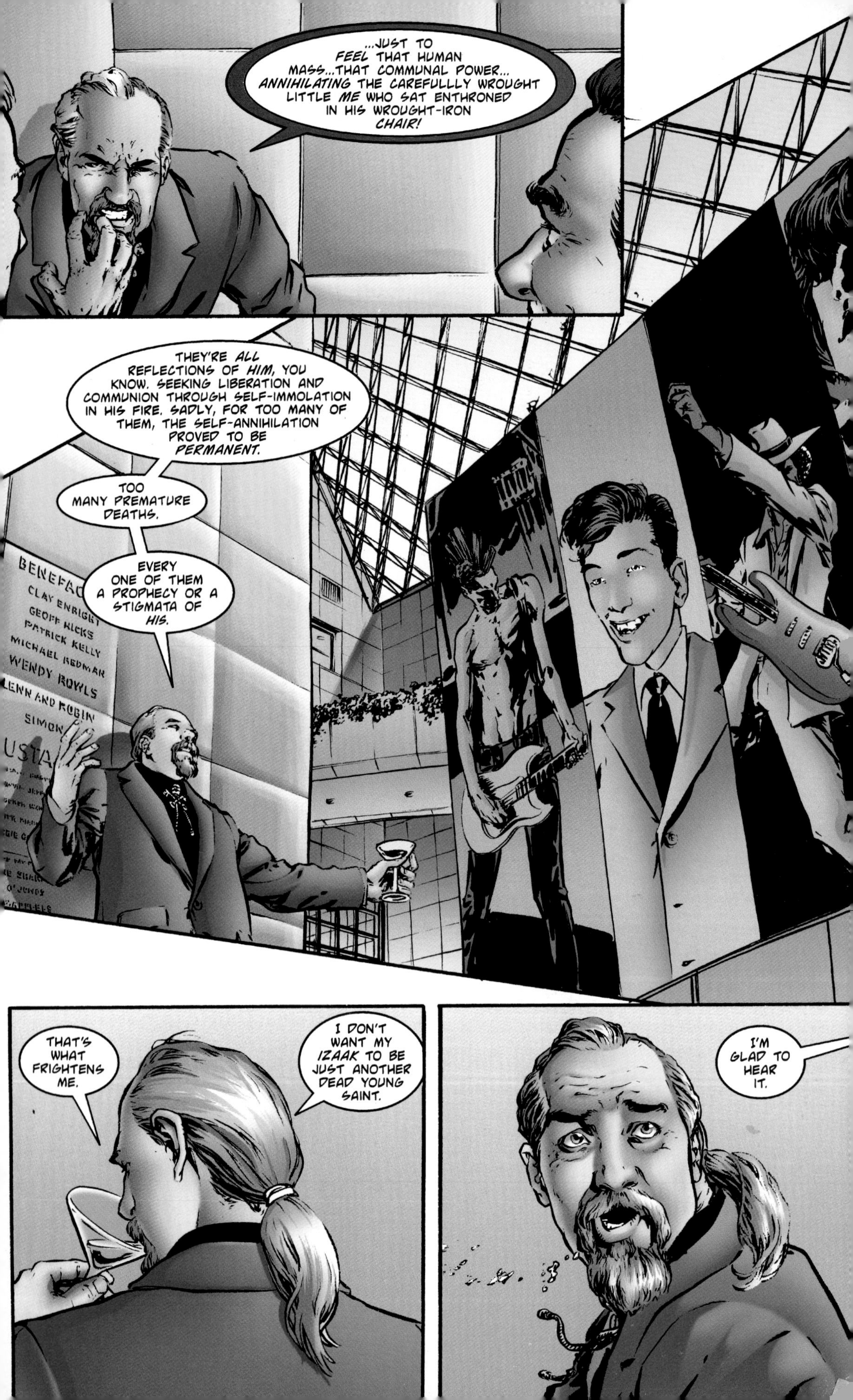

...JUST TO FEEL THAT HUMAN MASS...THAT COMMUNAL POWER... ANNIHILATING THE CAREFULLLY WROUGHT LITTLE ME WHO SAT ENTHRONED IN HIS WROUGHT-IRON CHAIR!
THEY'RE ALL REFLECTIONS OF HIM, YOU KNOW. SEEKING LIBERATION AND COMMUNION THROUGH SELF-IMMOLATION IN HIS FIRE. SADLY, FOR TOO MANY OF THEM, THE SELF-ANNIHILATION PROVED TO BE PERMANENT.
TOO MANY PREMATURE DEATHS.
EVERY ONE OF THEM A PROPHECY OR A STIGMATA OF HIS.
BENEFAC
CLAY ENRIGHT
GEOFF HICKS
PATRICK KELLY
MICHAEL REDMAN
WENDY ROWLS
LENN AND ROBIN
SIMON
USTA
THAT'S WHAT FRIGHTENS ME.
I DON'T WANT MY IZAAK TO BE JUST ANOTHER DEAD YOUNG SAINT.
I'M GLAD TO HEAR IT.

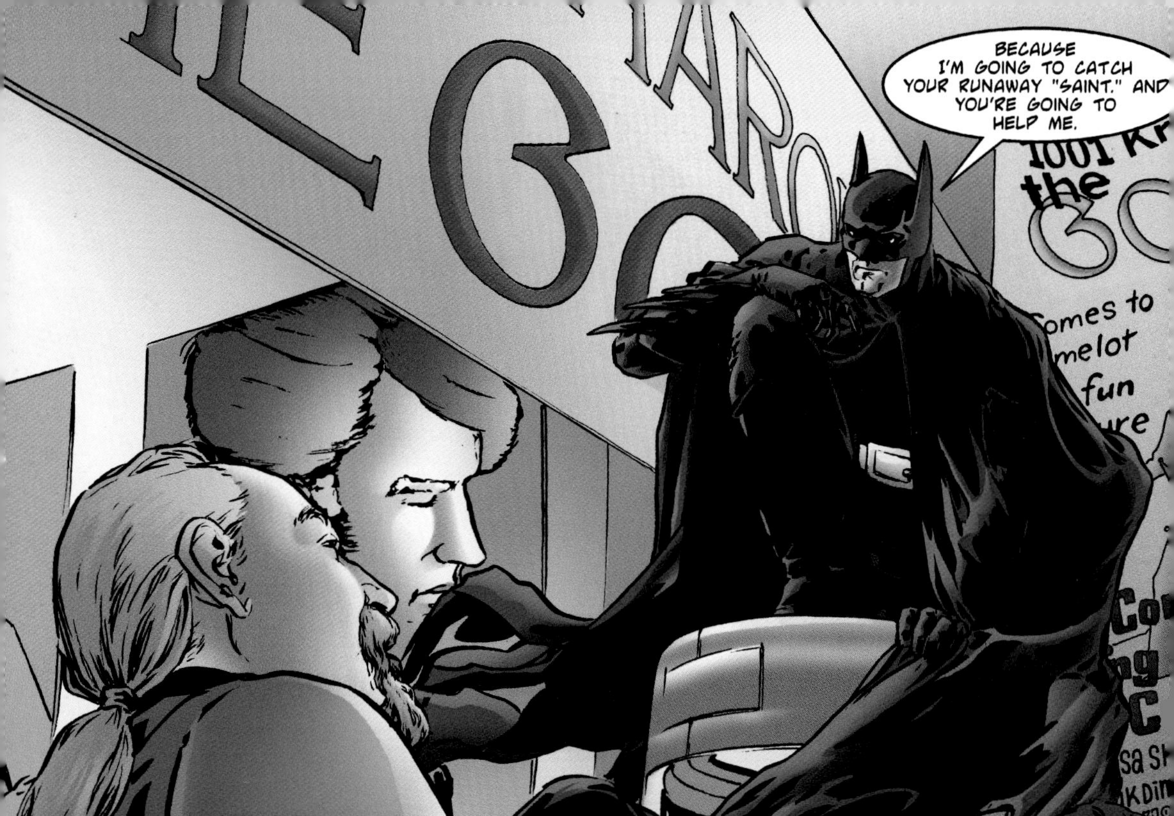
BECAUSE I'M GOING TO CATCH YOUR RUNAWAY "SAINT." AND YOU'RE GOING TO HELP ME.

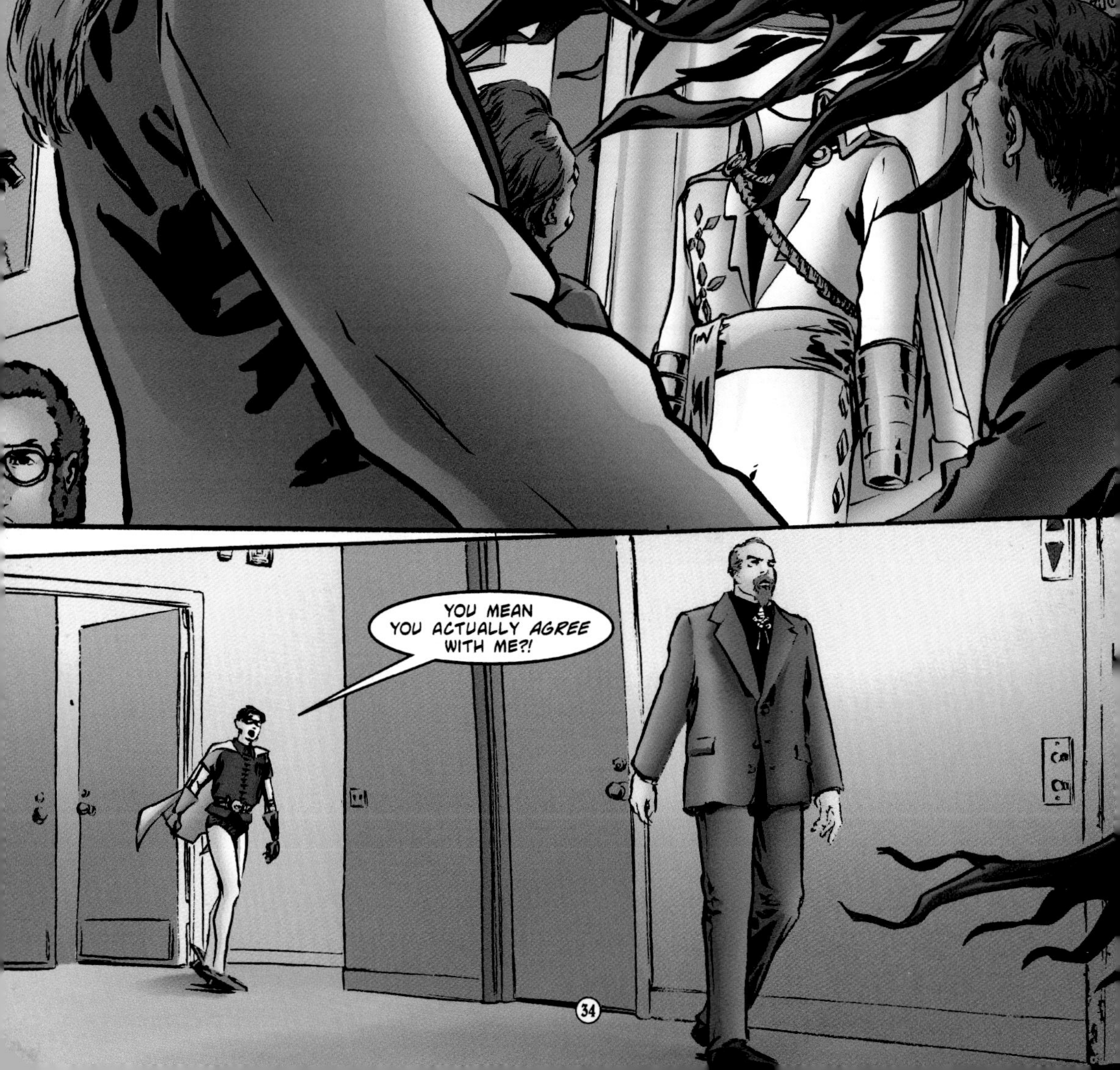
YOU MEAN YOU ACTUALLY AGREE WITH ME?!

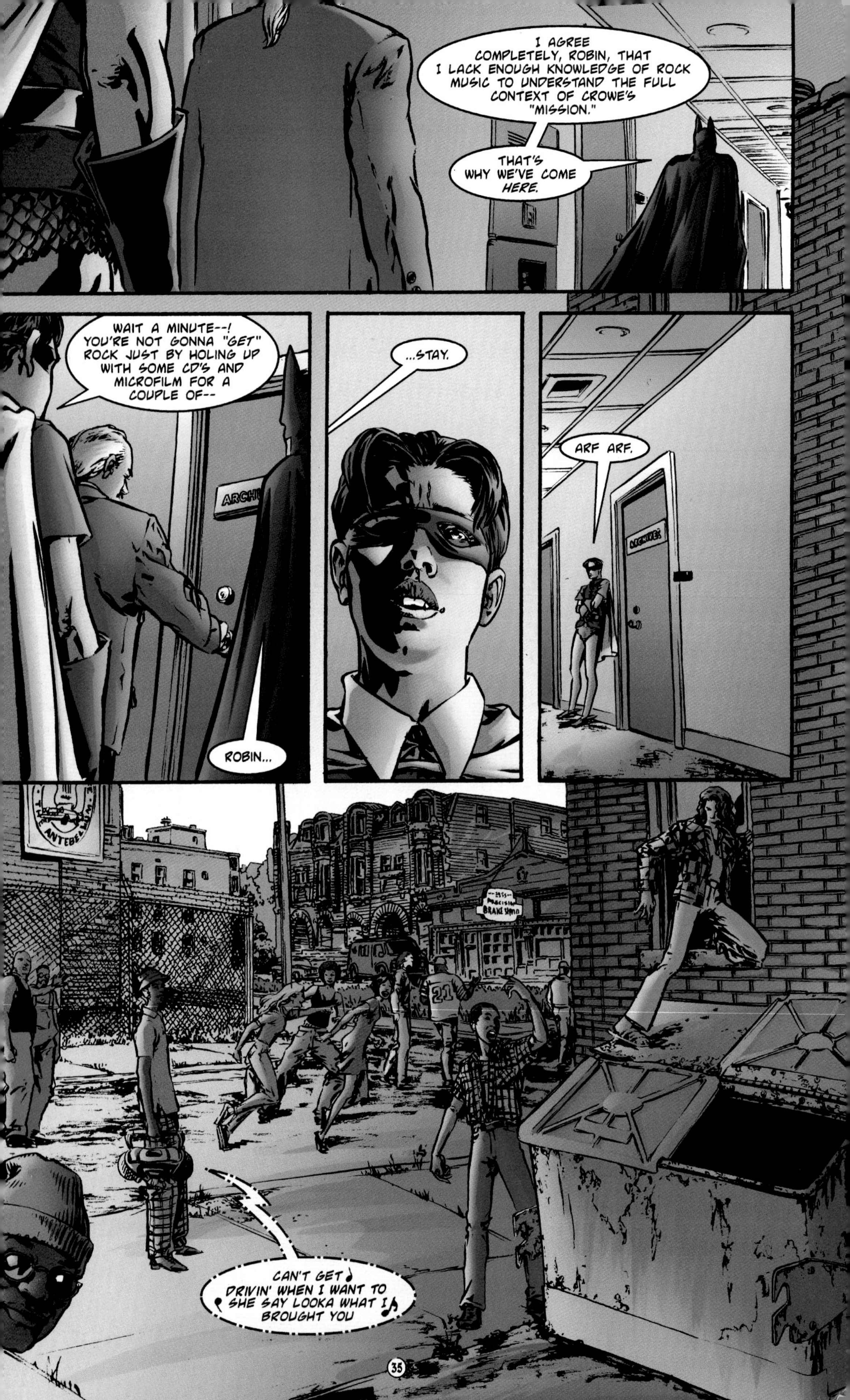
I AGREE COMPLETELY, ROBIN, THAT I LACK ENOUGH KNOWLEDGE OF ROCK MUSIC TO UNDERSTAND THE FULL CONTEXT OF CROWE'S "MISSION."
THAT'S WHY WE'VE COME HERE.
WAIT A MINUTE--! YOU'RE NOT GONNA "GET" ROCK JUST BY HOLING UP WITH SOME CD'S AND MICROFILM FOR A COUPLE OF--
ROBIN...
...STAY.
ARF ARF.
CAN'T GET DRIVIN' WHEN I WANT TO SHE SAY LOOKA WHAT I BROUGHT YOU

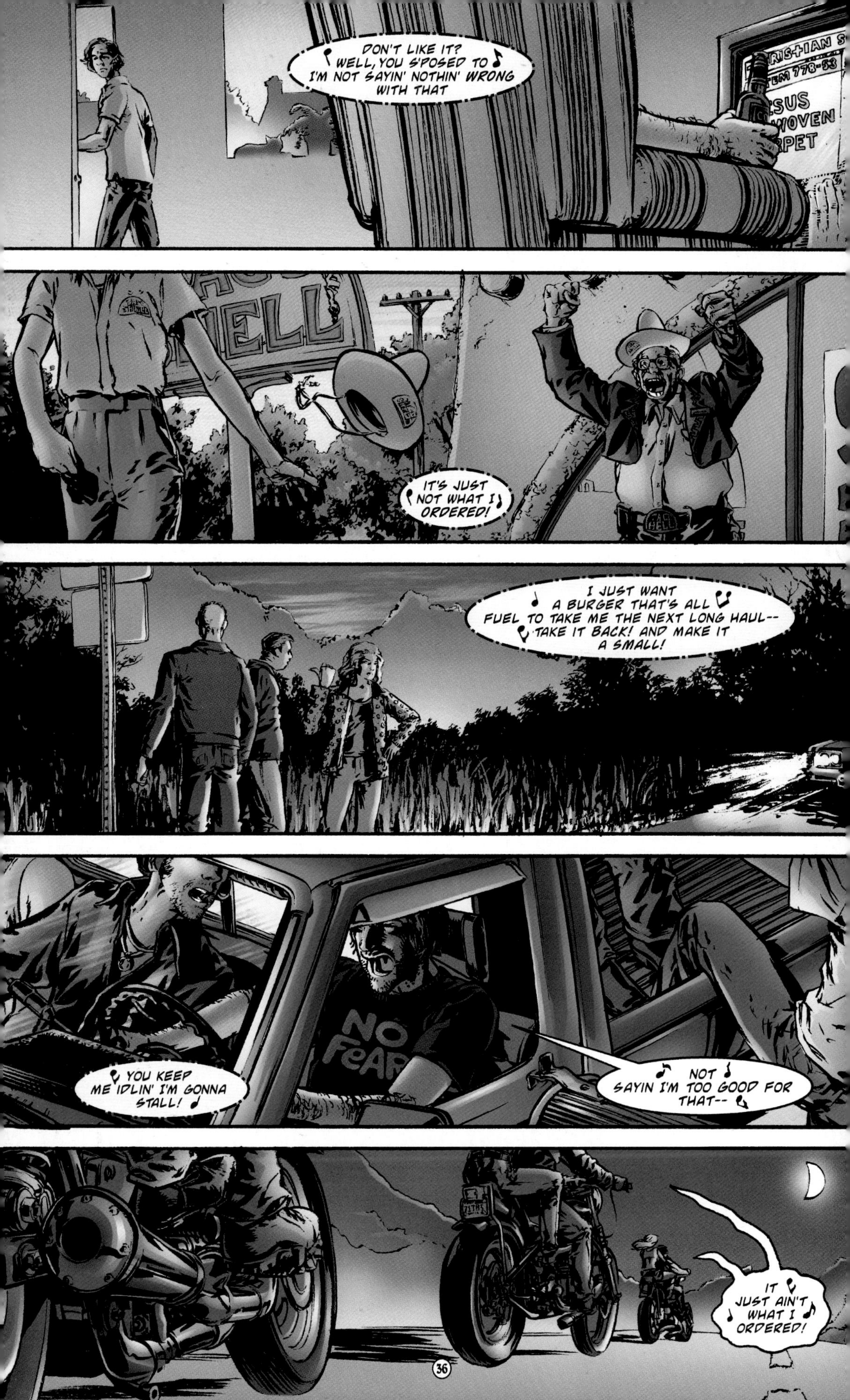
DON'T LIKE IT? WELL, YOU S'POSED TO I'M NOT SAYIN' NOTHIN' WRONG WITH THAT
IT'S JUST NOT WHAT I ORDERED!
I JUST WANT A BURGER THAT'S ALL FUEL TO TAKE ME THE NEXT LONG HAUL-- TAKE IT BACK! AND MAKE IT A SMALL!
YOU KEEP ME IDLIN' I'M GONNA STALL!
NOT SAYIN I'M TOO GOOD FOR THAT--
IT JUST AIN'T WHAT I ORDERED!

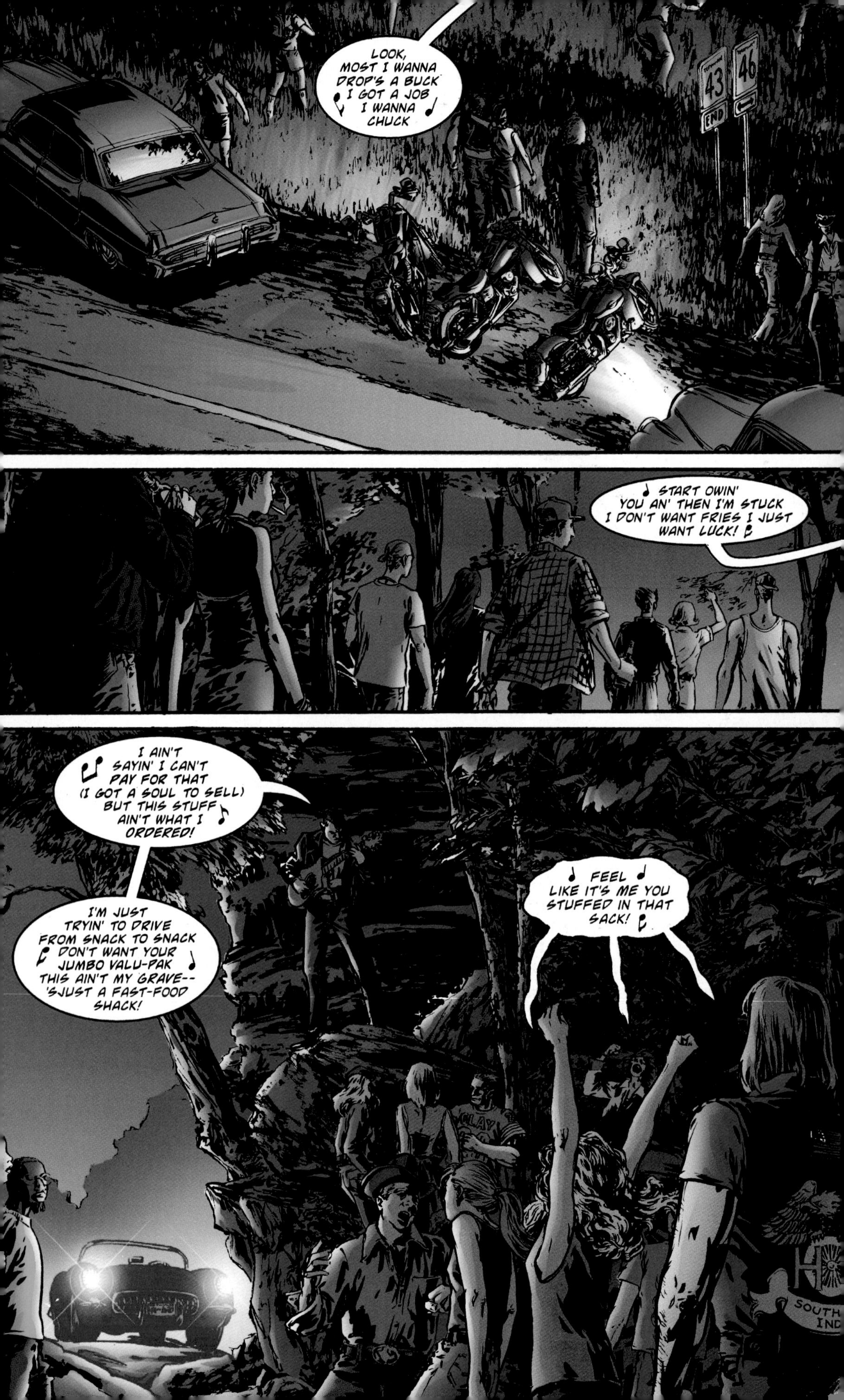
LOOK, MOST I WANNA DROP'S A BUCK I GOT A JOB I WANNA CHUCK
43
END
46
START OWIN' YOU AN' THEN I'M STUCK I DON'T WANT FRIES I JUST WANT LUCK!
I AIN'T SAYIN' I CAN'T PAY FOR THAT (I GOT A SOUL TO SELL) BUT THIS STUFF AIN'T WHAT I ORDERED!
I'M JUST TRYIN' TO DRIVE FROM SNACK TO SNACK DON'T WANT YOUR JUMBO VALU-PAK THIS AIN'T MY GRAVE-- 'SJUST A FAST-FOOD SHACK!
FEEL LIKE IT'S ME YOU STUFFED IN THAT SACK!

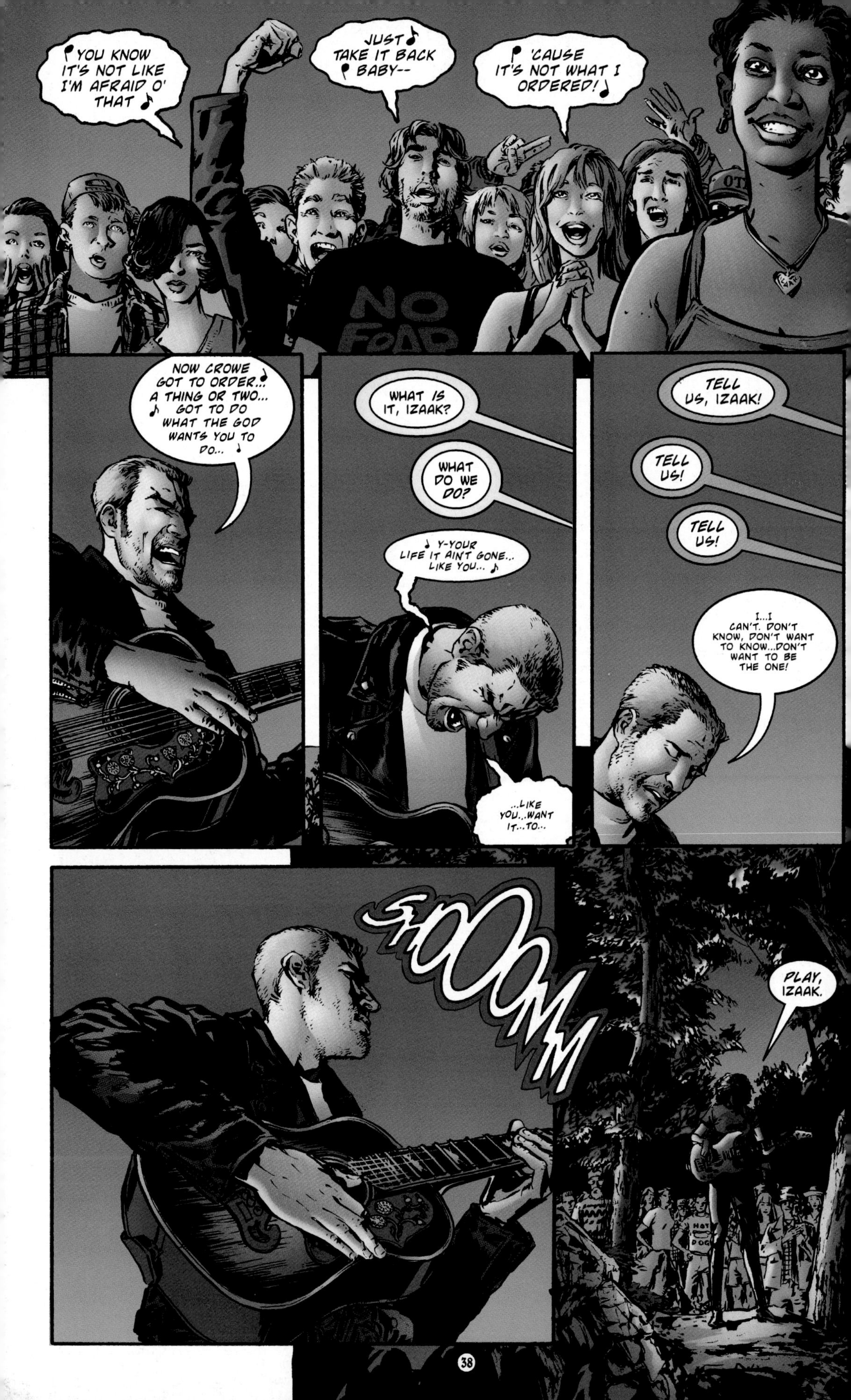
♪ YOU KNOW IT'S NOT LIKE I'M AFRAID O' THAT ♪
JUST ♪ TAKE IT BACK ♪ BABY--
♪ 'CAUSE IT'S NOT WHAT I ORDERED! ♪
NO FOOD
NOW CROWE GOT TO ORDER... ♪ A THING OR TWO... ♪ GOT TO DO WHAT THE GOD WANTS YOU TO DO... ♪
WHAT IS IT, IZAAK?
WHAT DO WE DO?
♪ Y-YOUR LIFE IT AIN'T GONE... LIKE YOU... ♪
...LIKE YOU...WANT IT...TO...
TELL US, IZAAK!
TELL US!
TELL US!
I...I CAN'T. DON'T KNOW, DON'T WANT TO KNOW...DON'T WANT TO BE THE ONE!
SKOOOMM
PLAY, IZAAK.
HOT DOG

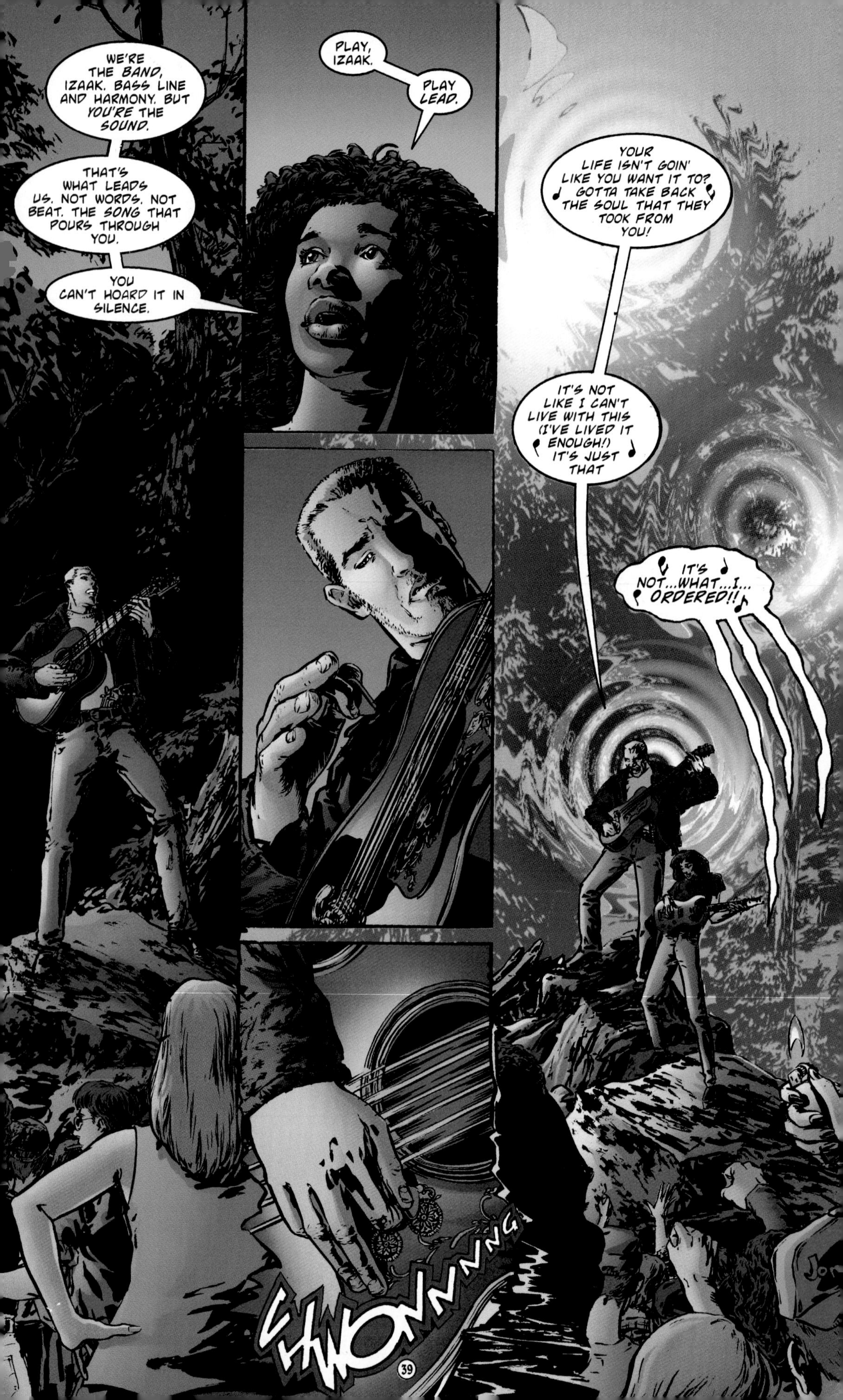
WE'RE THE *BAND*, IZAAK. BASS LINE AND HARMONY. BUT *YOU'RE* THE *SOUND*.
THAT'S WHAT LEADS US. NOT WORDS. NOT BEAT. THE *SONG* THAT POURS THROUGH YOU.
YOU CAN'T HOARD IT IN SILENCE.
PLAY, IZAAK.
PLAY *LEAD*.
YOUR LIFE ISN'T GOIN' LIKE YOU WANT IT TO? GOTTA TAKE BACK THE SOUL THAT THEY TOOK FROM YOU!
IT'S NOT LIKE I CAN'T LIVE WITH THIS (I'VE LIVED IT ENOUGH!) IT'S JUST THAT
IT'S NOT...WHAT...I... *ORDERED!!*
WHONNNNNG

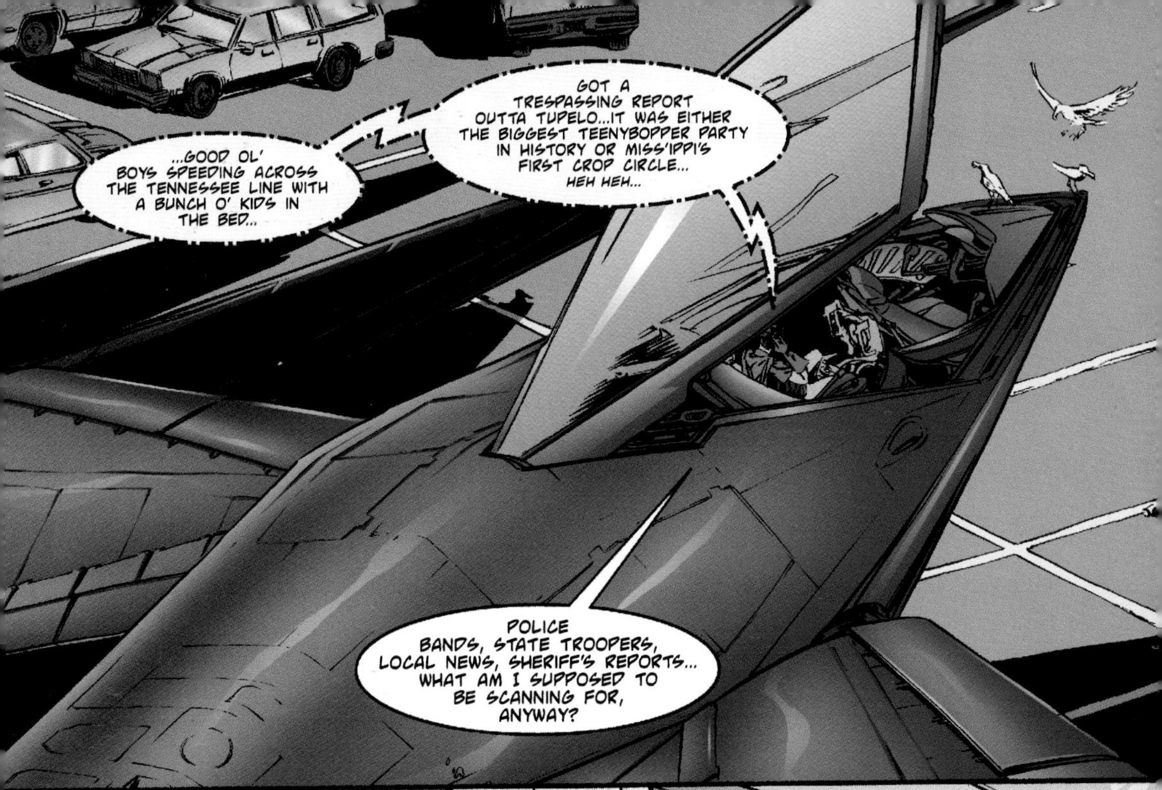

...GOOD OL' BOYS SPEEDING ACROSS THE TENNESSEE LINE WITH A BUNCH O' KIDS IN THE BED...
GOT A TRESPASSING REPORT OUTTA TUPELO...IT WAS EITHER THE BIGGEST TEENYBOPPER PARTY IN HISTORY OR MISS'IPPI'S FIRST CROP CIRCLE... HEH HEH...
POLICE BANDS, STATE TROOPERS, LOCAL NEWS, SHERIFF'S REPORTS... WHAT AM I SUPPOSED TO BE SCANNING FOR, ANYWAY?

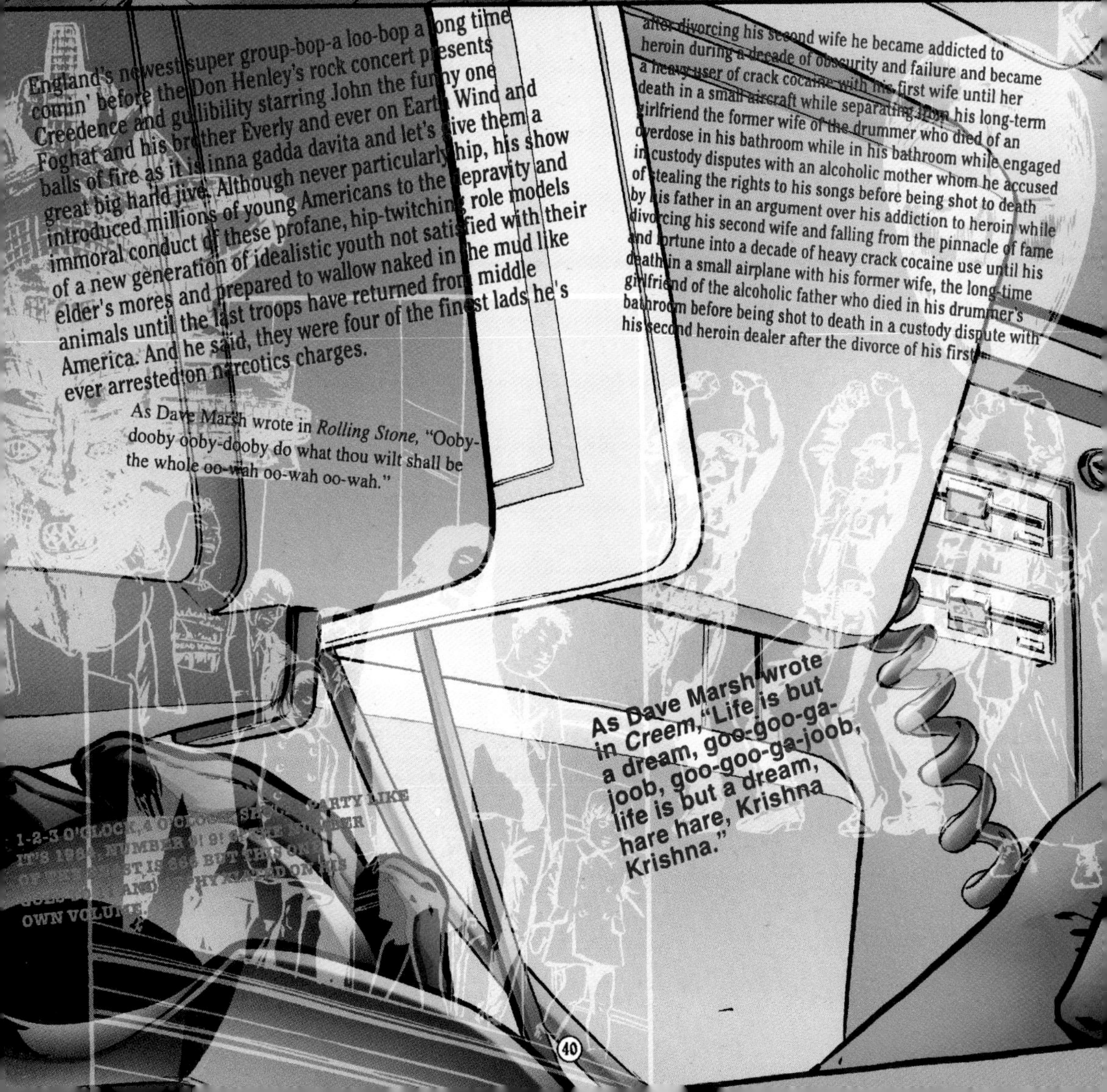

England's newest super group-bop-a loo-bop a long time comin' before the Don Henley's rock concert presents Creedence and gullibility starring John the funny one Foghat and his brother Everly and ever on Earth Wind and balls of fire as it is inna gadda davita and let's give them a great big hand jive. Although never particularly hip, his show introduced millions of young Americans to the depravity and immoral conduct of these profane, hip-twitching role models of a new generation of idealistic youth not satisfied with their elder's mores and prepared to wallow naked in the mud like animals until the last troops have returned from middle America. And he said, they were four of the finest lads he's ever arrested on narcotics charges.
As Dave Marsh wrote in Rolling Stone, "Ooby-dooby ooby-dooby do what thou wilt shall be the whole oo-wah oo-wah oo-wah."
after divorcing his second wife he became addicted to heroin during a decade of obscurity and failure and became a heavy user of crack cocaine with his first wife until her death in a small aircraft while separating from his long-term girlfriend the former wife of the drummer who died of an overdose in his bathroom while in his bathroom while engaged in custody disputes with an alcoholic mother whom he accused of stealing the rights to his songs before being shot to death by his father in an argument over his addiction to heroin while divorcing his second wife and falling from the pinnacle of fame and fortune into a decade of heavy crack cocaine use until his death in a small airplane with his former wife, the long-time girlfriend of the alcoholic father who died in his drummer's bathroom before being shot to death in a custody dispute with his second heroin dealer after the divorce of his first...
As Dave Marsh wrote in Creem, "Life is but a dream, goo-goo-ga-joob, goo-goo-ga-joob, a dream, life is but a dream, hare hare, Krishna Krishna."
PARTY LIKE
1-2-3 O'CLOCK, 4 O'CLOCK
OWN VOLUME.

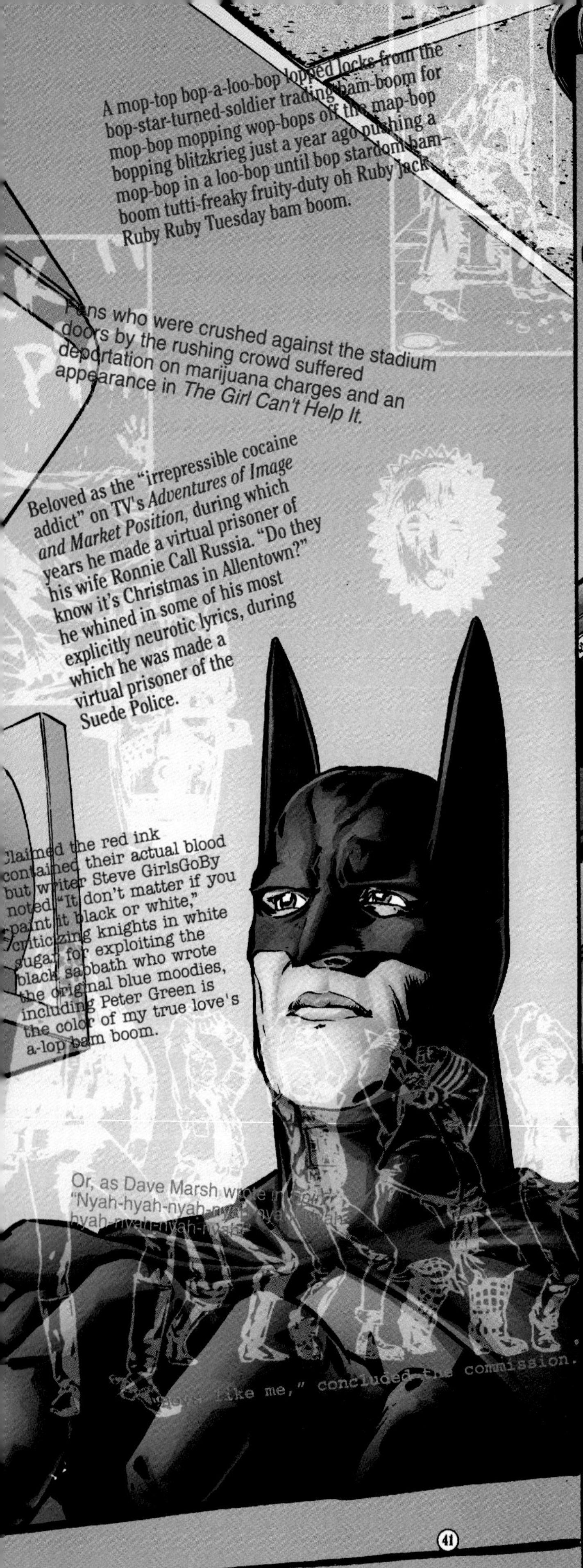
A mop-top bop-a-loo-bop lopped locks from the bop-star-turned-soldier trading bam-boom for mop-bop mopping wop-bops off the map-bop bopping blitzkrieg just a year ago pushing a mop-bop in a loo-bop until bop stardom bam-boom tutti-freaky fruity-duty oh Ruby Jack Ruby Ruby Tuesday bam boom.
Fans who were crushed against the stadium doors by the rushing crowd suffered deportation on marijuana charges and an appearance in *The Girl Can't Help It.*
Beloved as the "irrepressible cocaine addict" on TV's *Adventures of Image and Market Position,* during which years he made a virtual prisoner of his wife Ronnie Call Russia. "Do they know it's Christmas in Allentown?" he whined in some of his most explicitly neurotic lyrics, during which he was made a virtual prisoner of the Suede Police.
Claimed the red ink contained their actual blood but writer Steve GirlsGoBy noted, "It don't matter if you paint it black or white," criticizing knights in white sugar for exploiting the black sabbath who wrote the original blue moodies, including Peter Green is the color of my true love's a-lop bam boom.
Or, as Dave Marsh wrote
"Nyah-hyah-nyah-
like me," concluded the commission.
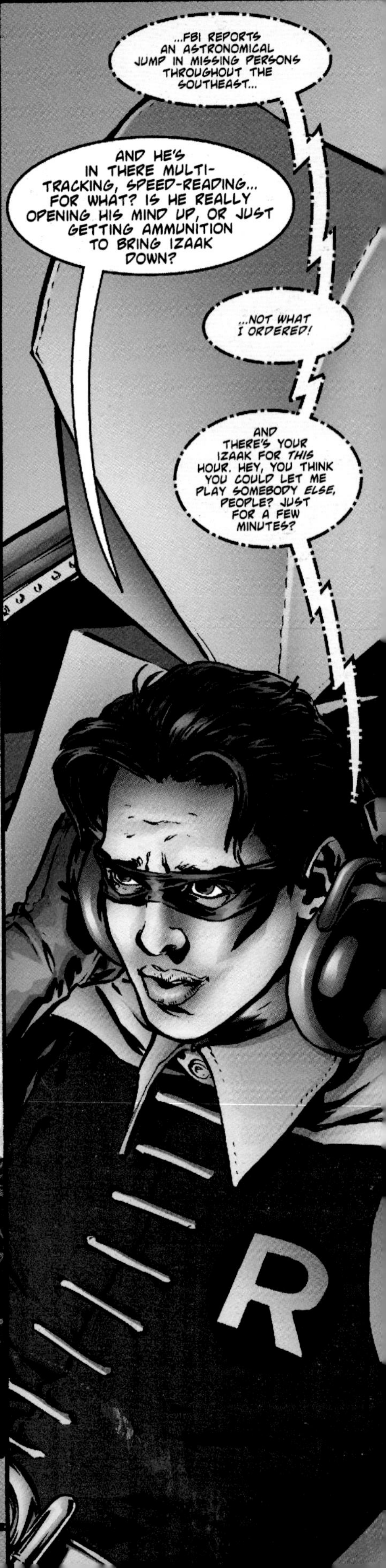
...FBI REPORTS AN ASTRONOMICAL JUMP IN MISSING PERSONS THROUGHOUT THE SOUTHEAST...
AND HE'S IN THERE MULTI-TRACKING, SPEED-READING... FOR WHAT? IS HE REALLY OPENING HIS MIND UP, OR JUST GETTING AMMUNITION TO BRING IZAAK DOWN?
...NOT WHAT I ORDERED!
AND THERE'S YOUR IZAAK FOR *THIS* HOUR. HEY, YOU THINK YOU COULD LET ME PLAY SOMEBODY *ELSE,* PEOPLE? JUST FOR A FEW MINUTES?

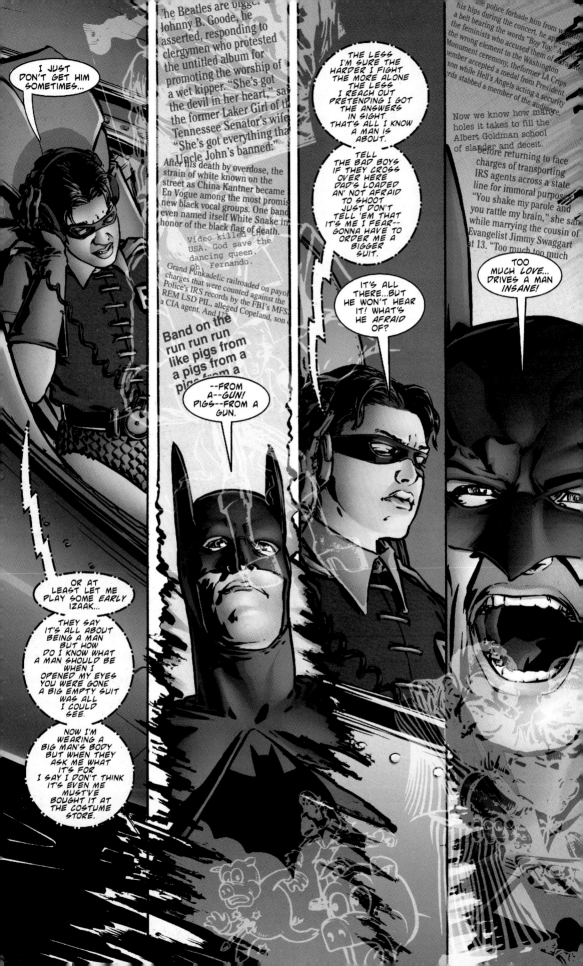

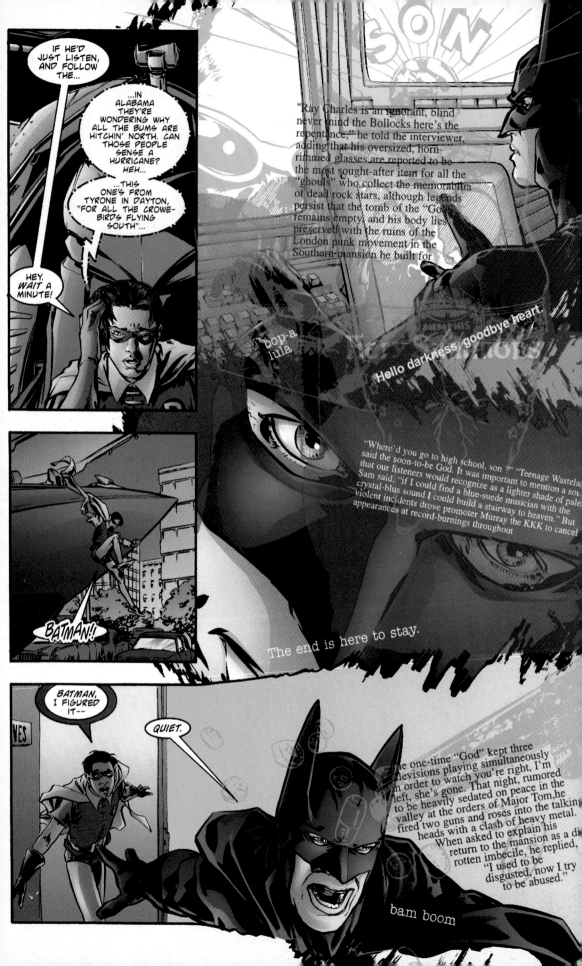

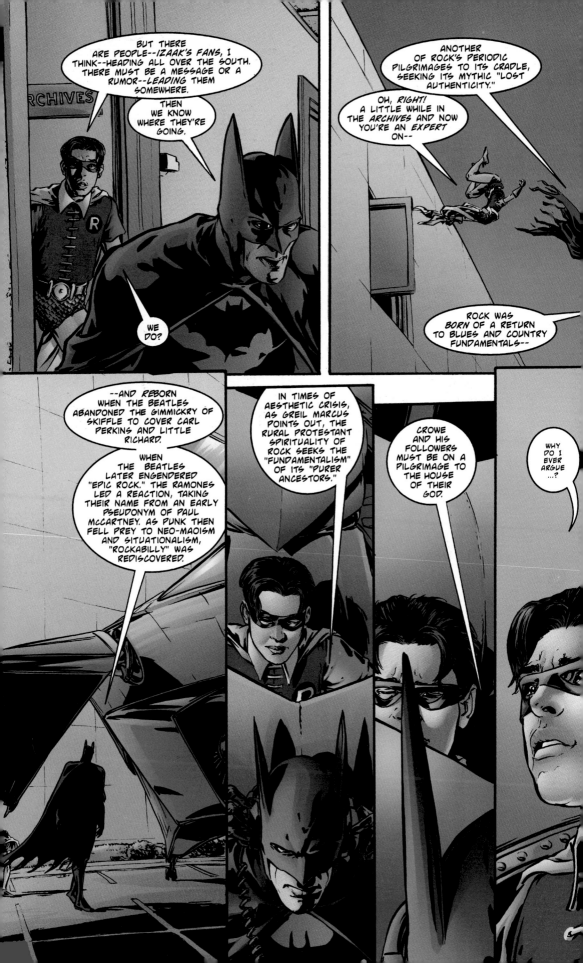

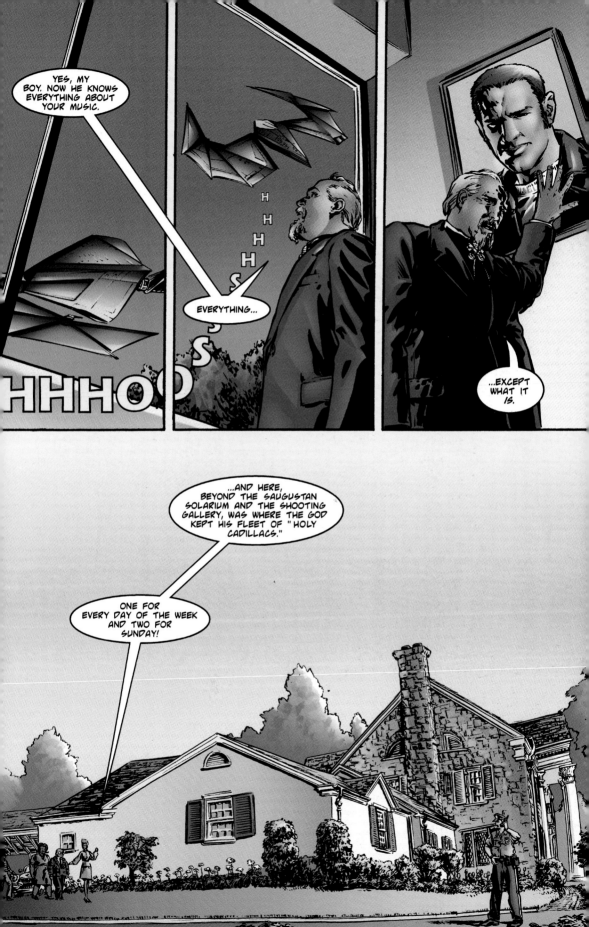

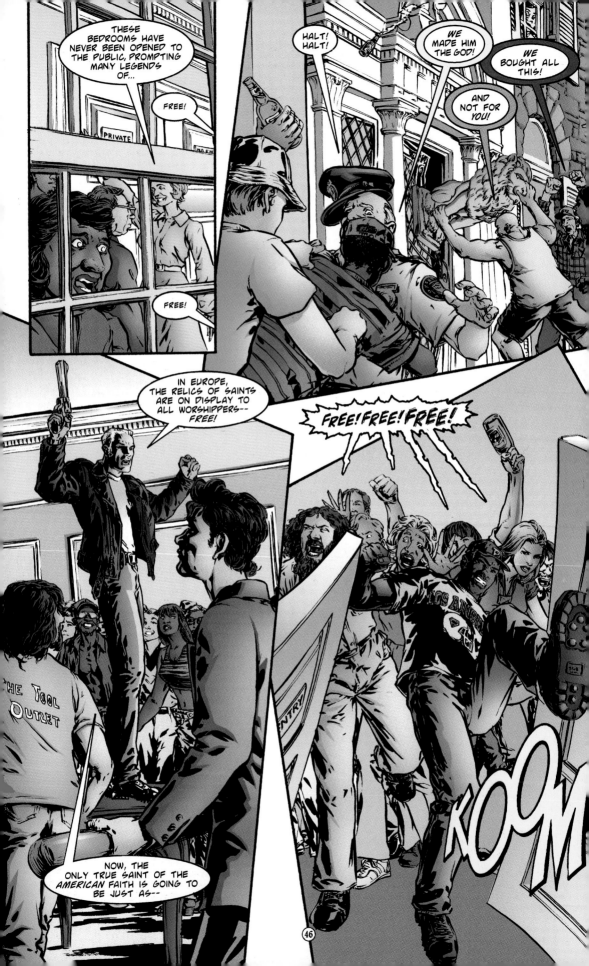

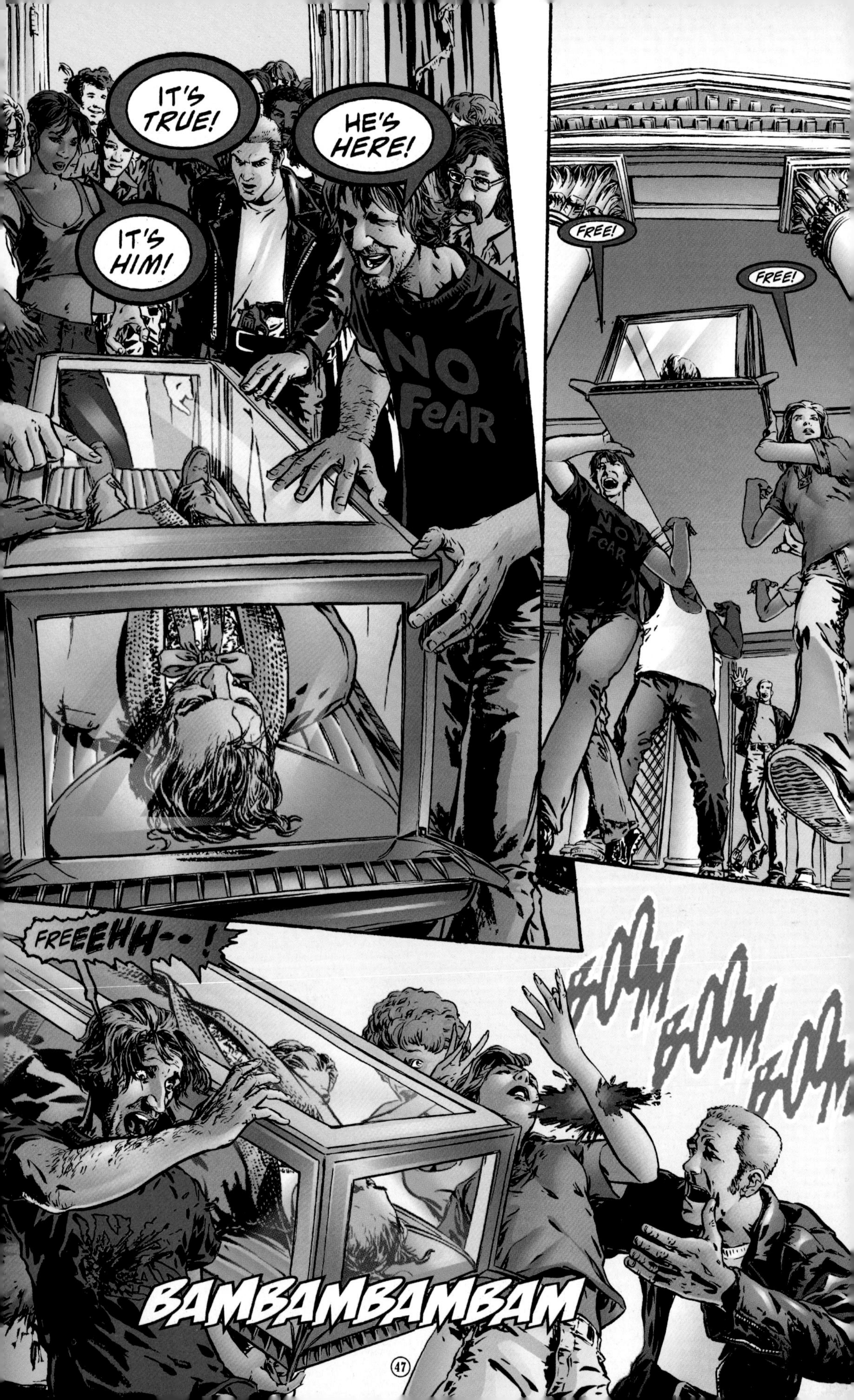
IT'S TRUE!
HE'S HERE!
IT'S HIM!
NO FEAR
FREE!
FREE!
FREEEHH--!
BOOM
BOOM
BOOM
BAMBAMBAMBAM

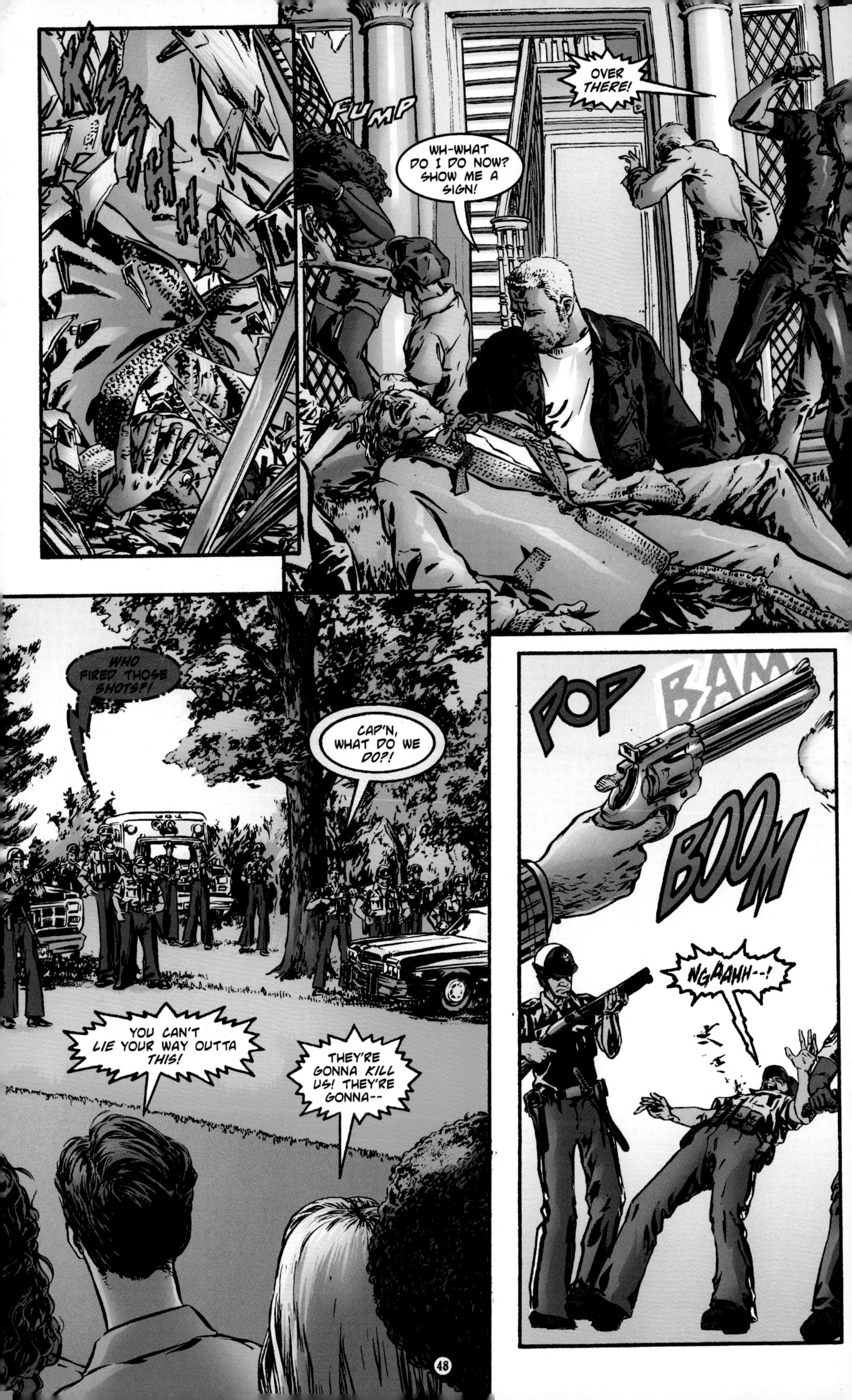
FUMP
WH-WHAT DO I DO NOW? SHOW ME A SIGN!
OVER THERE!
WHO FIRED THOSE SHOTS?!
CAP'N, WHAT DO WE DO?!
YOU CAN'T LIE YOUR WAY OUTTA THIS!
THEY'RE GONNA KILL US! THEY'RE GONNA--
POP
BAM
BOOM
NGAAHH--!

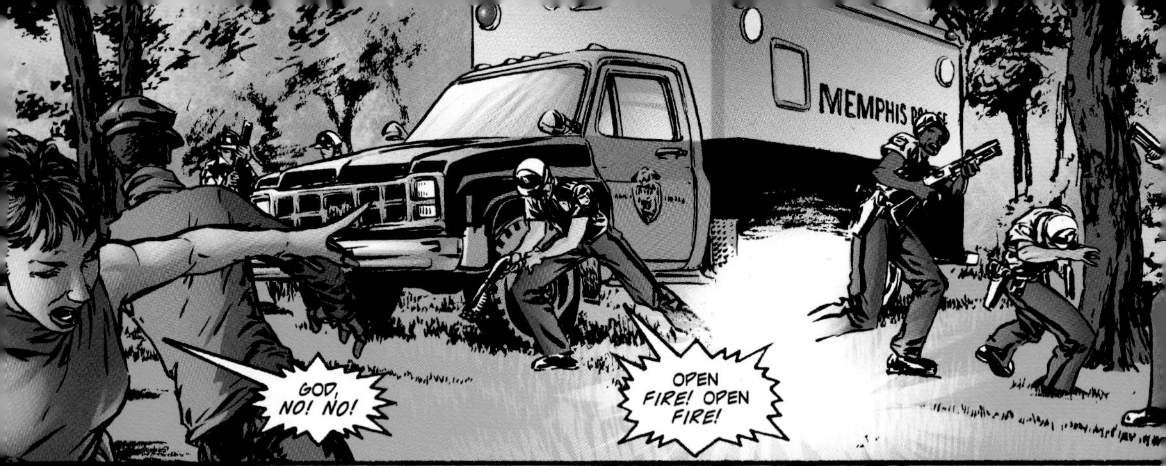
MEMPHIS
GOD, NO! NO!
OPEN FIRE! OPEN FIRE!
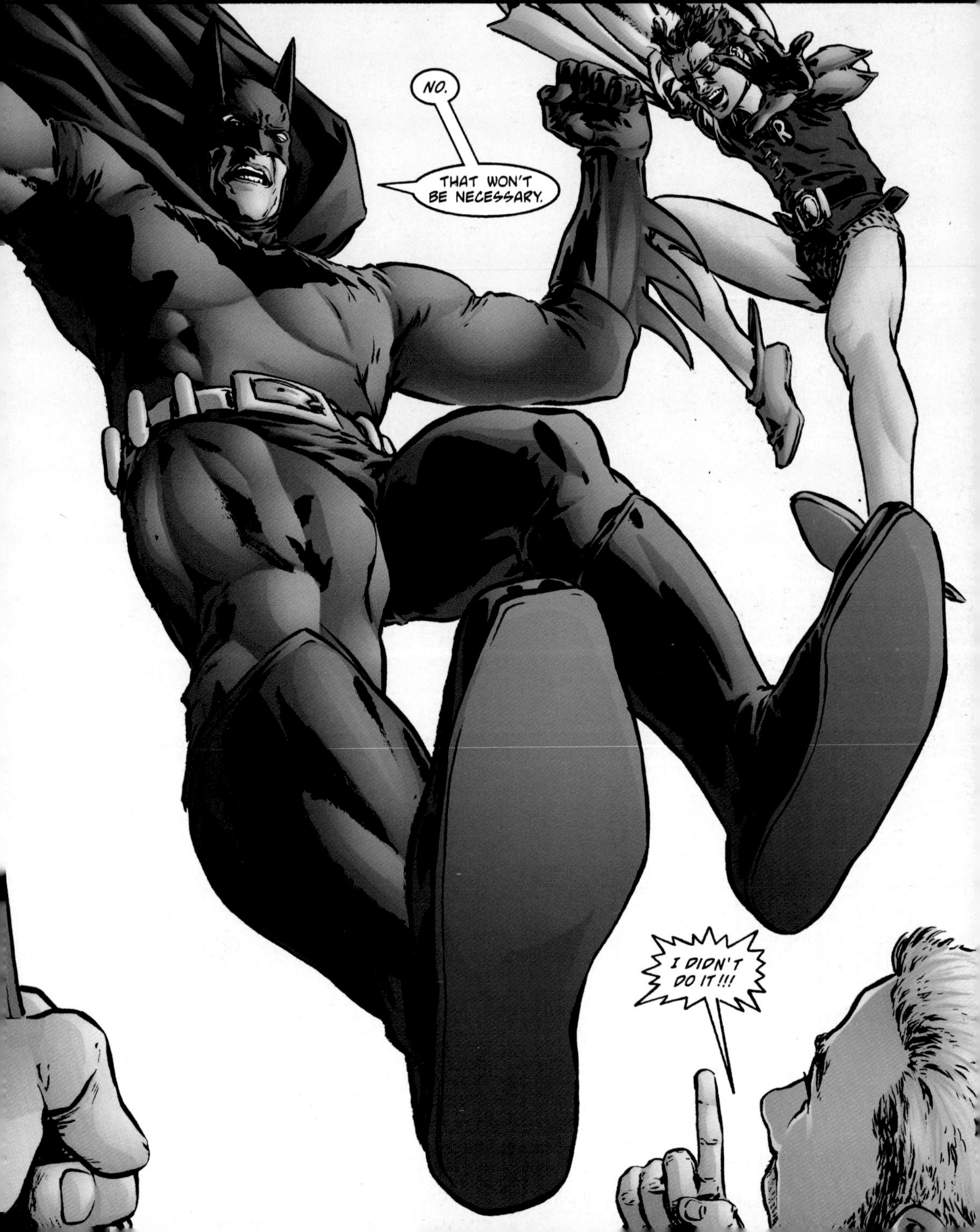
NO.
THAT WON'T BE NECESSARY.
I DIDN'T DO IT!!!

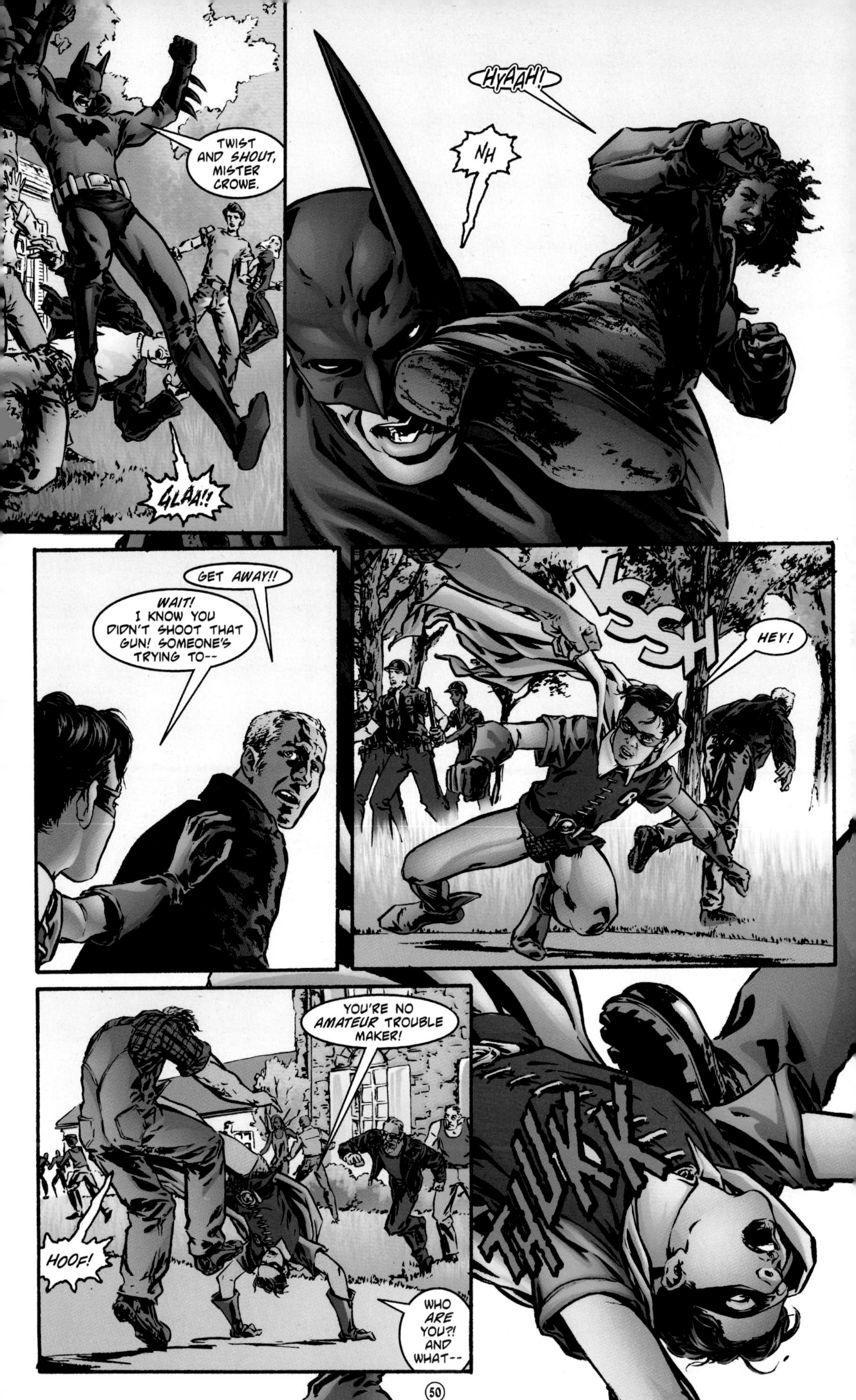
TWIST AND SHOUT, MISTER CROWE.
GLAA!!
HYAAH!
NH
GET AWAY!!
WAIT! I KNOW YOU DIDN'T SHOOT THAT GUN! SOMEONE'S TRYING TO--
VSSH
HEY!
YOU'RE NO AMATEUR TROUBLE MAKER!
HOOF!
WHO ARE YOU?! AND WHAT--
THUKK

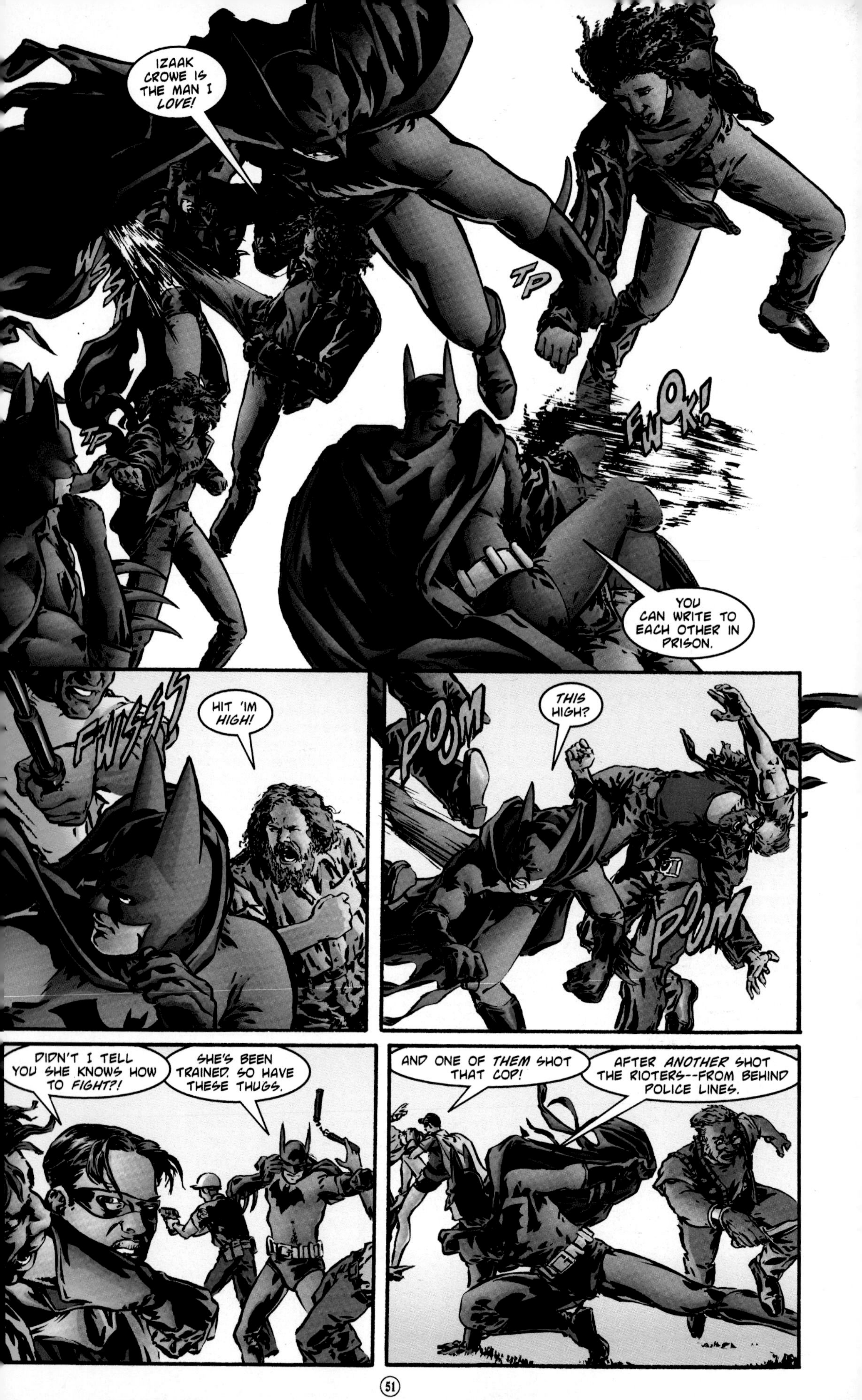
IZAAK CROWE IS THE MAN I *LOVE!*
TP
TP
FWOK!
YOU CAN WRITE TO EACH OTHER IN PRISON.
HIT 'IM *HIGH!*
POOM
THIS HIGH?
POOM
DIDN'T I TELL YOU SHE KNOWS HOW TO *FIGHT?!*
SHE'S BEEN TRAINED. SO HAVE THESE THUGS.
AND ONE OF *THEM* SHOT THAT COP!
AFTER *ANOTHER* SHOT THE RIOTERS--FROM BEHIND POLICE LINES.

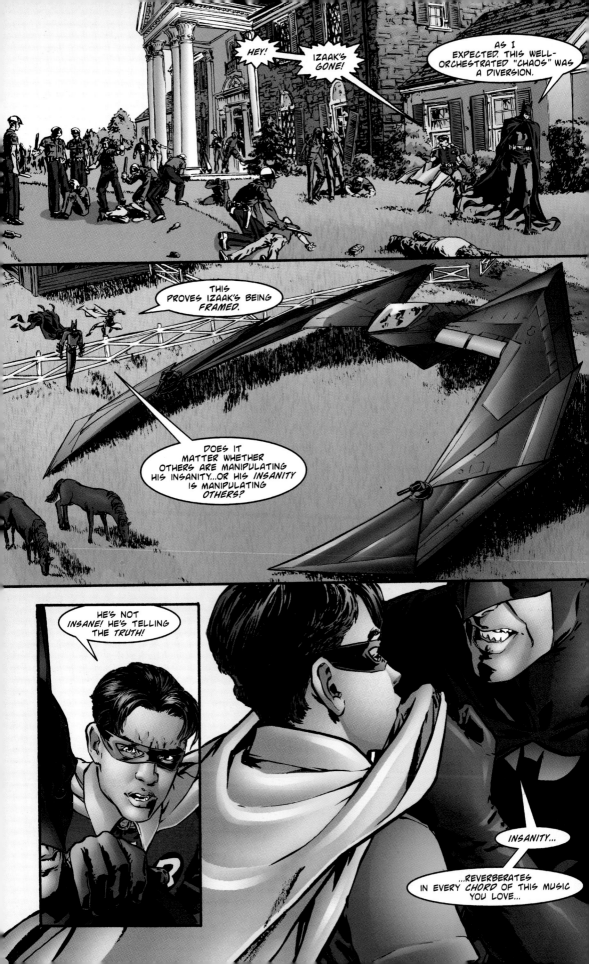

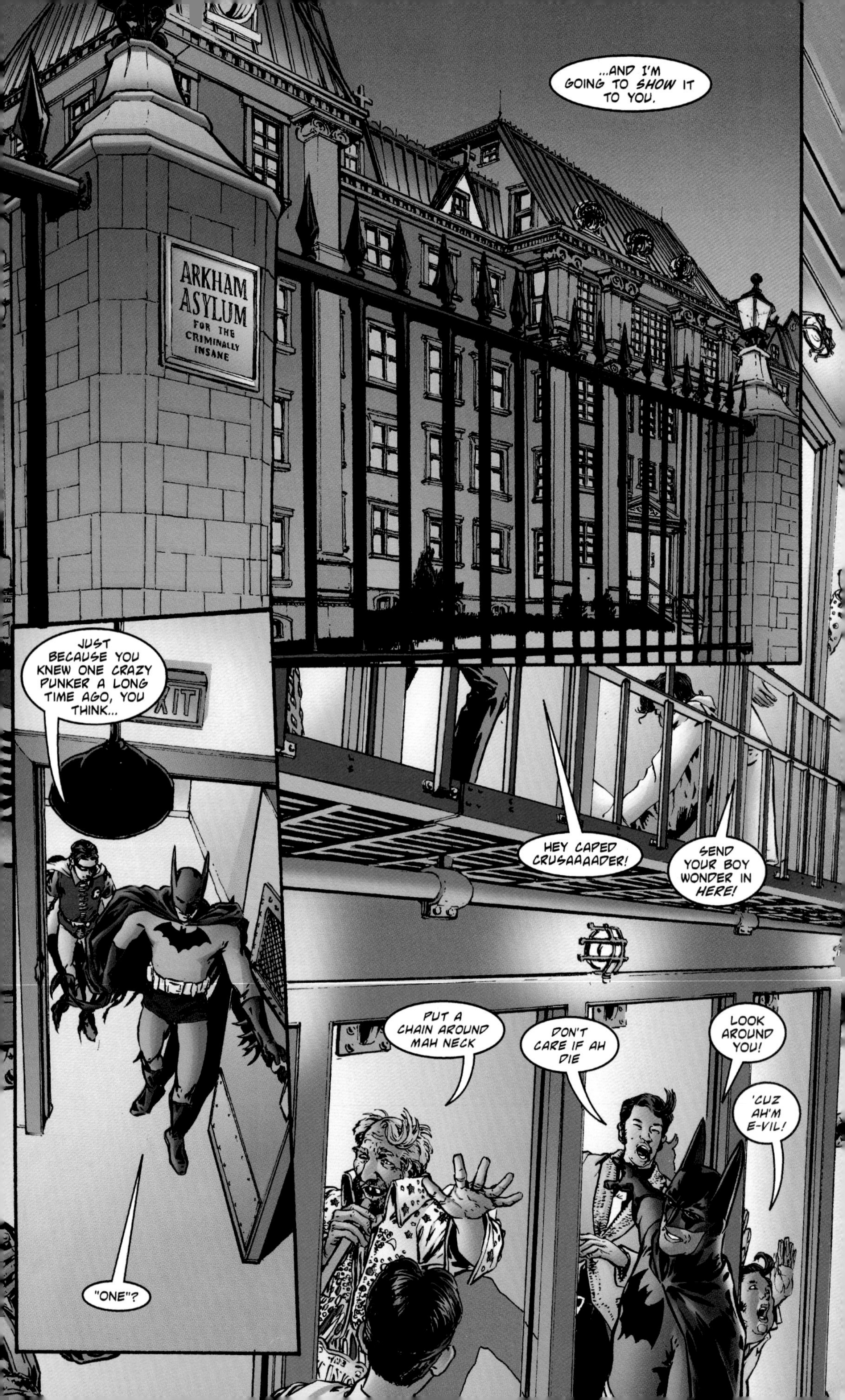
ARKHAM ASYLUM FOR THE CRIMINALLY INSANE
...AND I'M GOING TO *SHOW* IT TO YOU.
JUST BECAUSE YOU KNEW ONE CRAZY PUNKER A LONG TIME AGO, YOU THINK...
"ONE"?
HEY CAPED CRUSAAAAADER!
SEND YOUR BOY WONDER IN *HERE!*
PUT A CHAIN AROUND MAH NECK
DON'T CARE IF AH DIE
LOOK AROUND YOU!
'CUZ AH'M E-VIL!

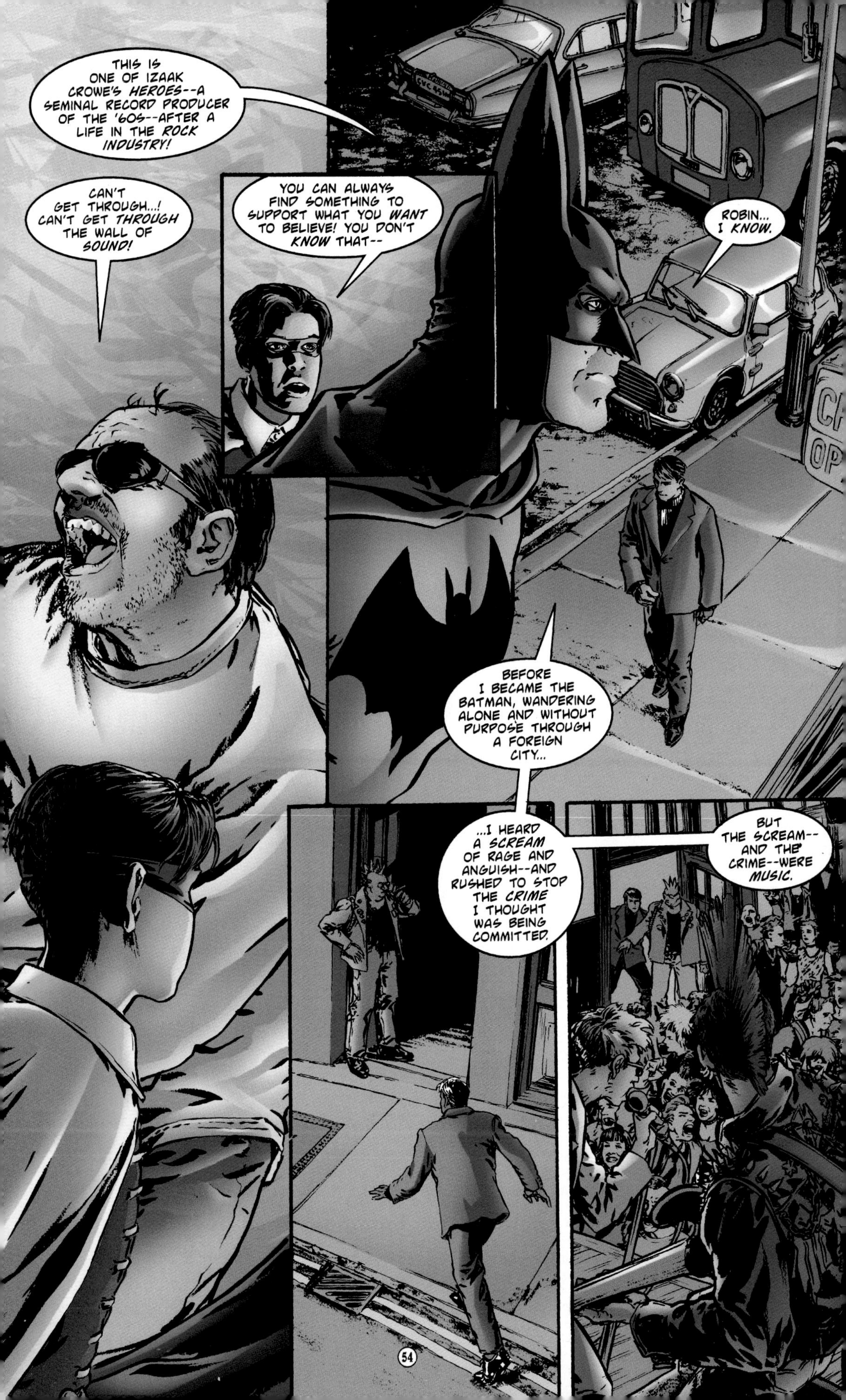
THIS IS ONE OF IZAAK CROWE'S *HEROES*--A SEMINAL RECORD PRODUCER OF THE '60S--AFTER A LIFE IN THE *ROCK INDUSTRY!*
CAN'T GET THROUGH...! CAN'T GET *THROUGH* THE WALL OF *SOUND!*
YOU CAN ALWAYS FIND SOMETHING TO SUPPORT WHAT YOU *WANT* TO BELIEVE! YOU DON'T *KNOW* THAT--
ROBIN... I *KNOW.*
BEFORE I BECAME THE BATMAN, WANDERING ALONE AND WITHOUT PURPOSE THROUGH A FOREIGN CITY...
...I HEARD A *SCREAM* OF RAGE AND ANGUISH--AND RUSHED TO STOP THE *CRIME* I THOUGHT WAS BEING COMMITTED.
BUT THE SCREAM--AND THE CRIME--WERE *MUSIC.*

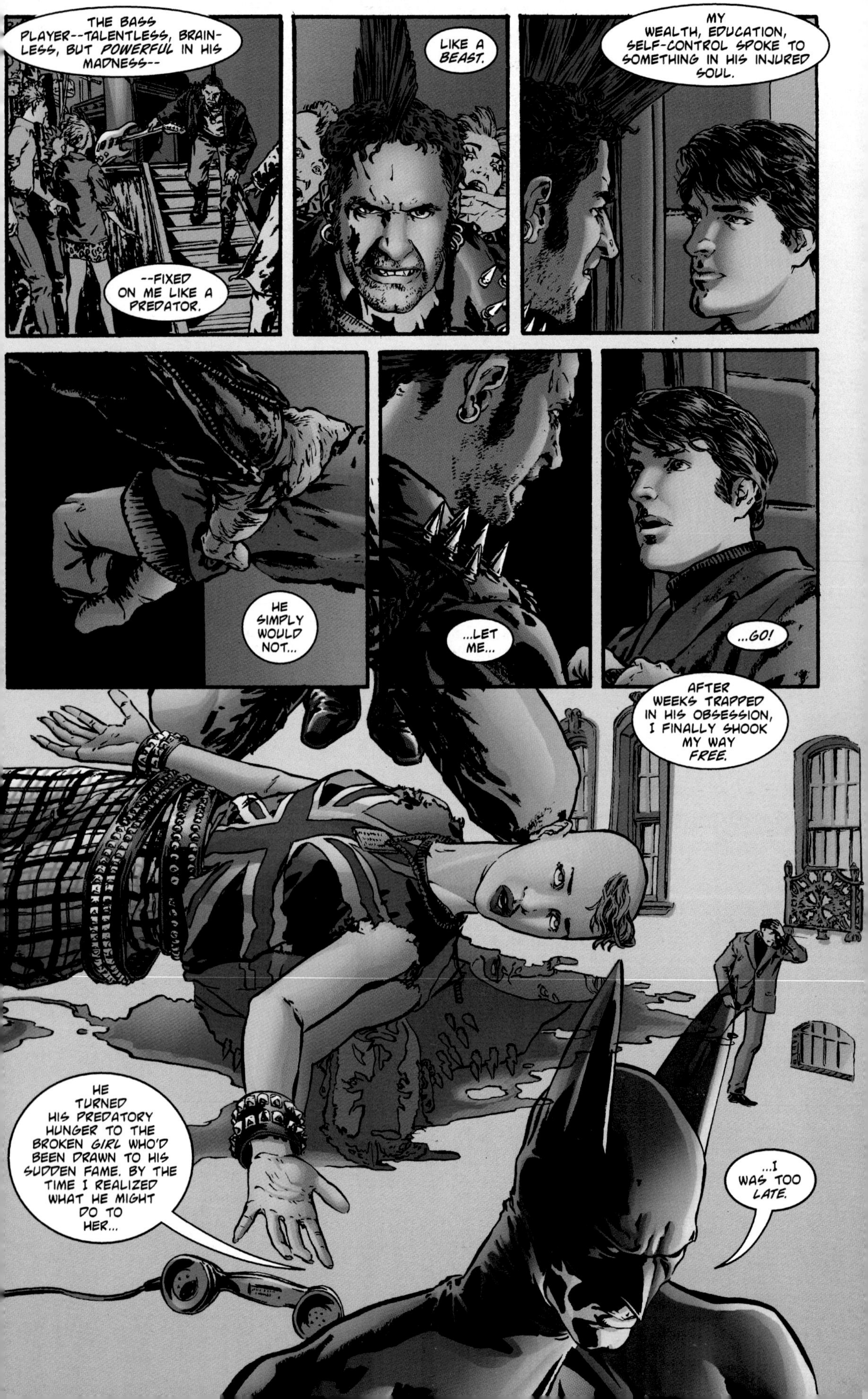
THE BASS PLAYER--TALENTLESS, BRAINLESS, BUT POWERFUL IN HIS MADNESS--
--FIXED ON ME LIKE A PREDATOR.
LIKE A BEAST.
MY WEALTH, EDUCATION, SELF-CONTROL SPOKE TO SOMETHING IN HIS INJURED SOUL.
HE SIMPLY WOULD NOT...
...LET ME...
...GO!
AFTER WEEKS TRAPPED IN HIS OBSESSION, I FINALLY SHOOK MY WAY FREE.
HE TURNED HIS PREDATORY HUNGER TO THE BROKEN GIRL WHO'D BEEN DRAWN TO HIS SUDDEN FAME. BY THE TIME I REALIZED WHAT HE MIGHT DO TO HER...
...I WAS TOO LATE.

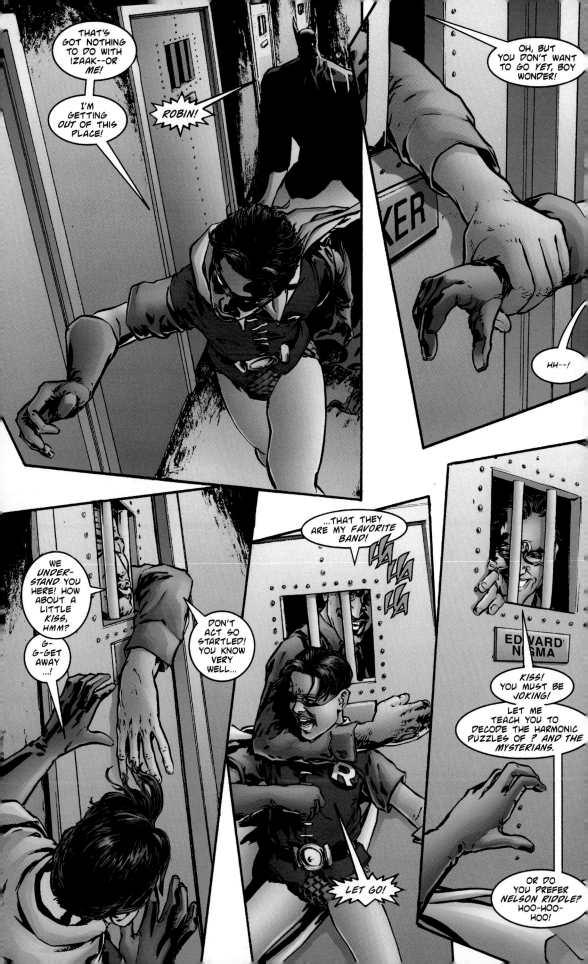

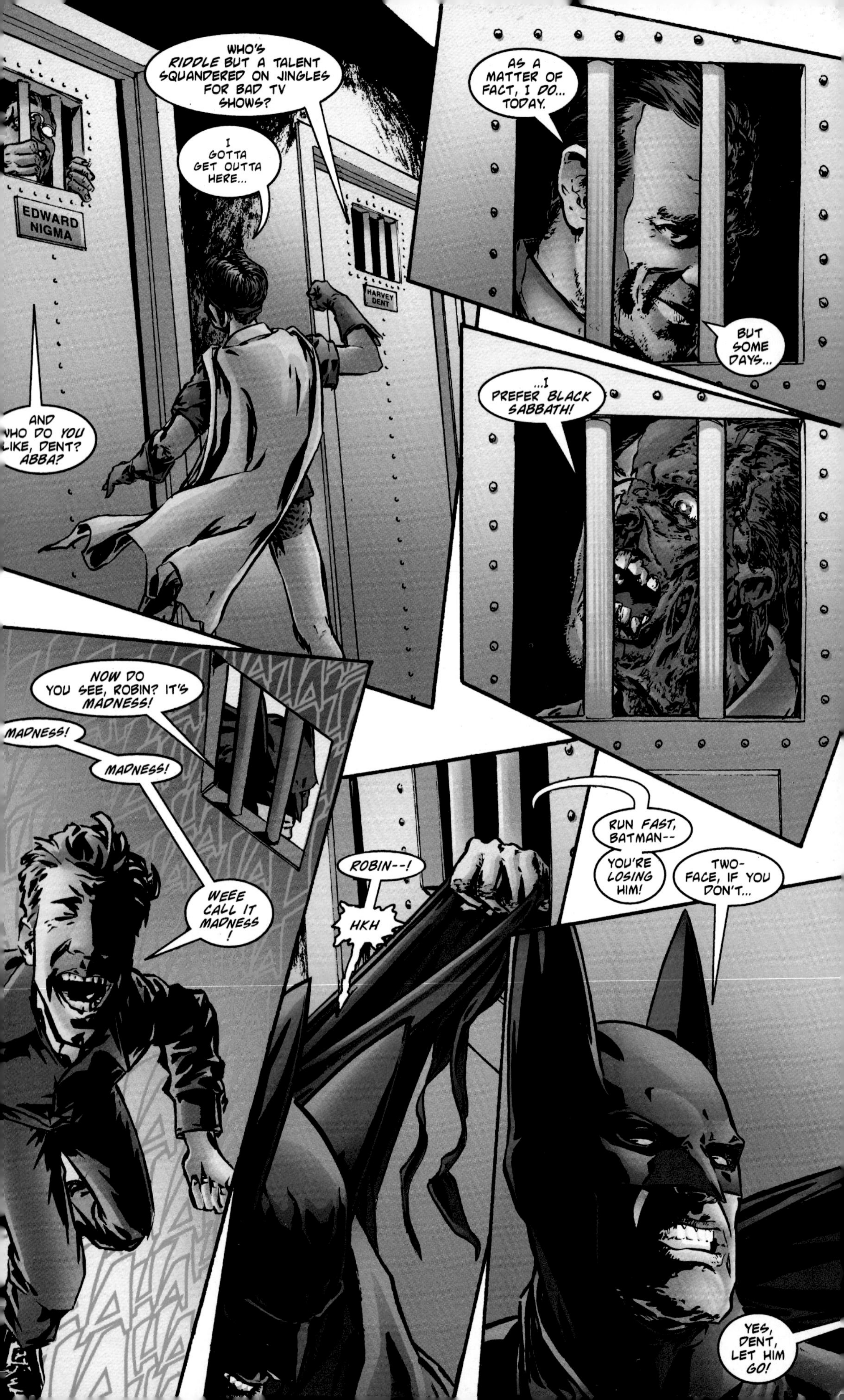
WHO'S RIDDLE BUT A TALENT SQUANDERED ON JINGLES FOR BAD TV SHOWS?
I GOTTA GET OUTTA HERE...
EDWARD NIGMA
HARVEY DENT
AND WHO DO YOU LIKE, DENT? ABBA?
AS A MATTER OF FACT, I DO... TODAY.
BUT SOME DAYS...
...I PREFER BLACK SABBATH!
NOW DO YOU SEE, ROBIN? IT'S MADNESS!
MADNESS!
MADNESS!
WEEE CALL IT MADNESS!
ROBIN--!
HKH
RUN FAST, BATMAN--
YOU'RE LOSING HIM!
TWO-FACE, IF YOU DON'T...
YES, DENT, LET HIM GO!

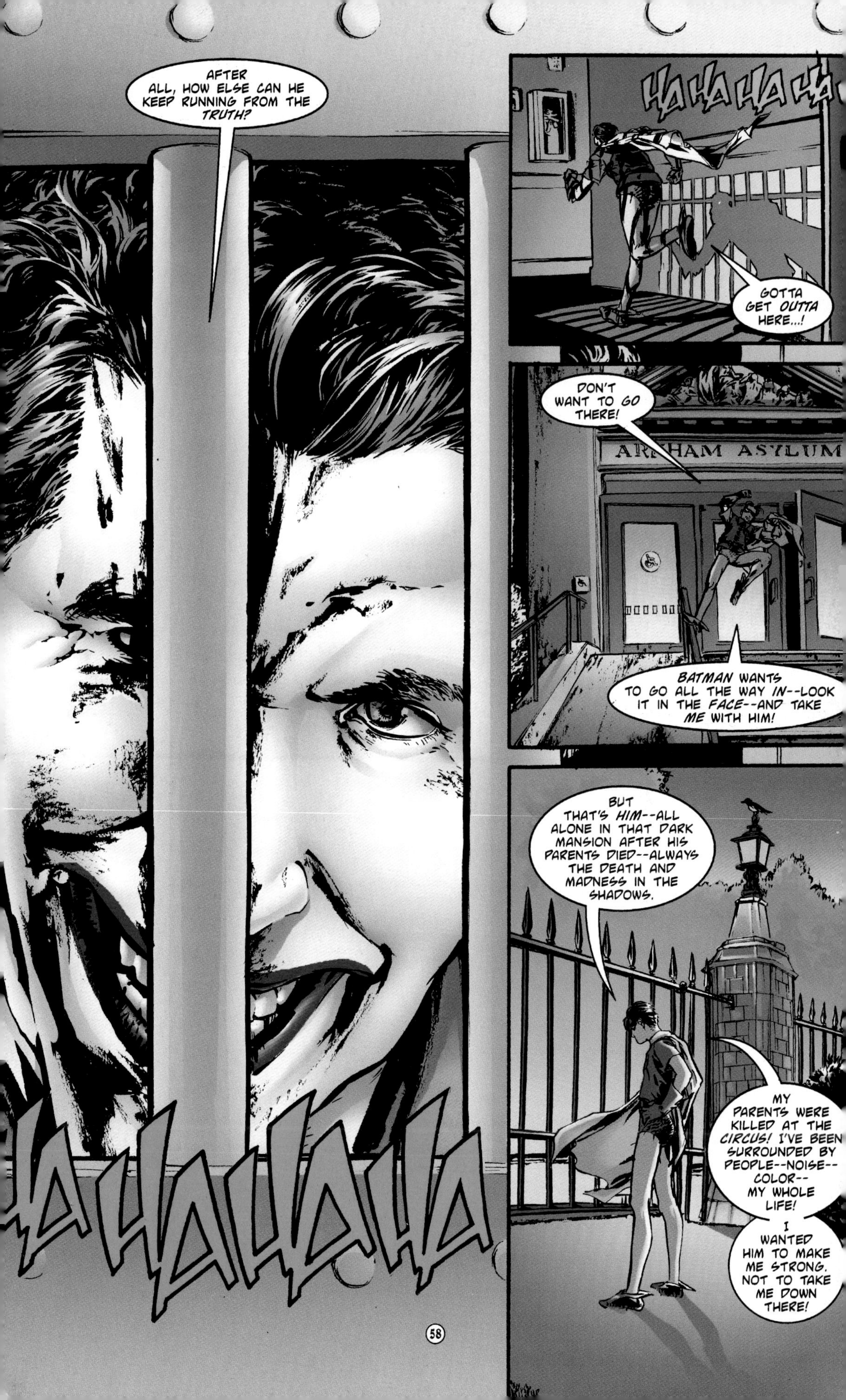
AFTER ALL, HOW ELSE CAN HE KEEP RUNNING FROM THE *TRUTH?*
HA HA HA HA HA
HA HA HA HA HA
GOTTA GET *OUTTA* HERE...!
DON'T WANT TO GO THERE!
ARKHAM ASYLUM
BATMAN WANTS TO GO ALL THE WAY *IN*--LOOK IT IN THE *FACE*--AND TAKE *ME* WITH HIM!
BUT THAT'S *HIM*--ALL ALONE IN THAT DARK MANSION AFTER HIS PARENTS DIED--ALWAYS THE DEATH AND MADNESS IN THE SHADOWS.
MY PARENTS WERE KILLED AT THE *CIRCUS!* I'VE BEEN SURROUNDED BY PEOPLE--NOISE--COLOR--MY WHOLE LIFE!
I WANTED HIM TO MAKE ME STRONG. NOT TO TAKE ME DOWN THERE!

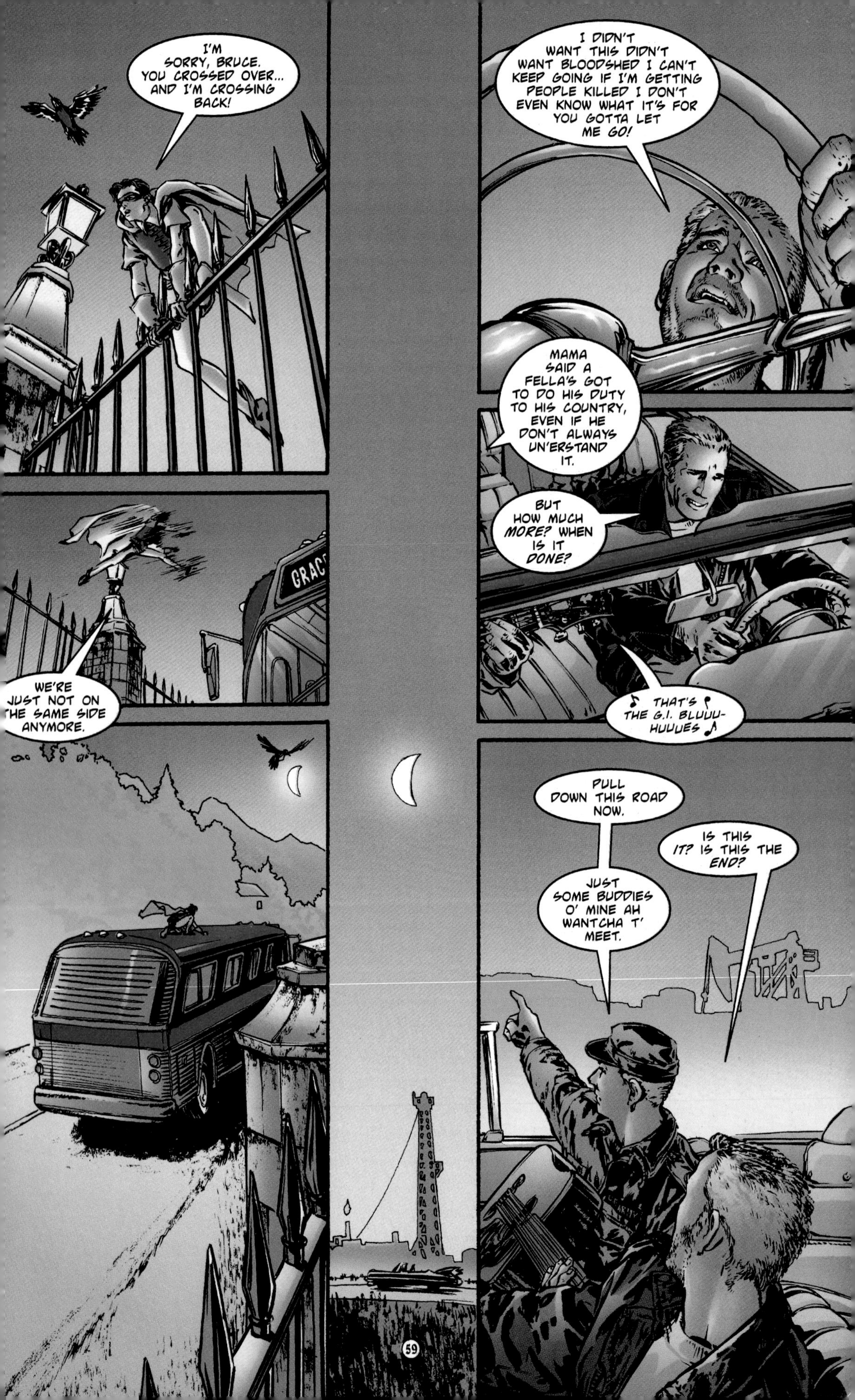
I'M SORRY, BRUCE. YOU CROSSED OVER... AND I'M CROSSING BACK!
I DIDN'T WANT THIS DIDN'T WANT BLOODSHED I CAN'T KEEP GOING IF I'M GETTING PEOPLE KILLED I DON'T EVEN KNOW WHAT IT'S FOR YOU GOTTA LET ME GO!
WE'RE JUST NOT ON THE SAME SIDE ANYMORE.
MAMA SAID A FELLA'S GOT TO DO HIS DUTY TO HIS COUNTRY, EVEN IF HE DON'T ALWAYS UN'ERSTAND IT.
BUT HOW MUCH *MORE?* WHEN IS IT *DONE?*
♪ THAT'S THE G.I. BLUUU-HUUUES ♪
PULL DOWN THIS ROAD NOW.
JUST SOME BUDDIES O' MINE AH WANTCHA T' MEET.
IS THIS *IT?* IS THIS THE *END?*

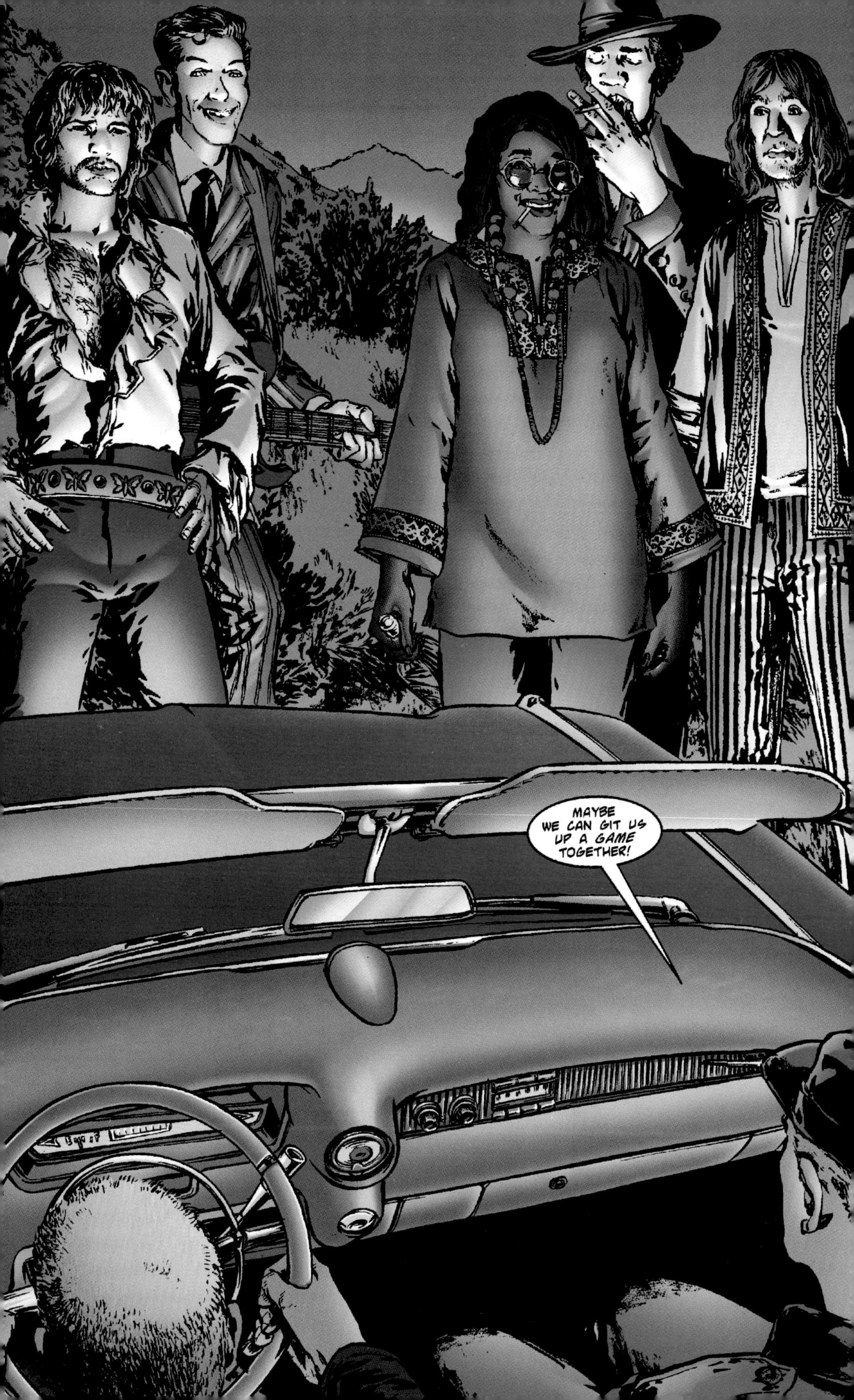
MAYBE WE CAN GIT US UP A GAME TOGETHER!

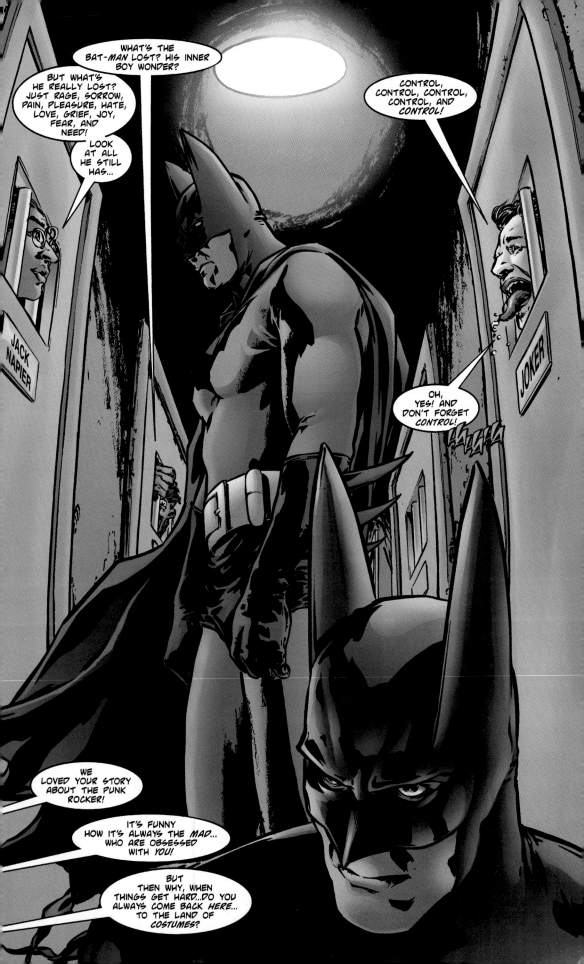

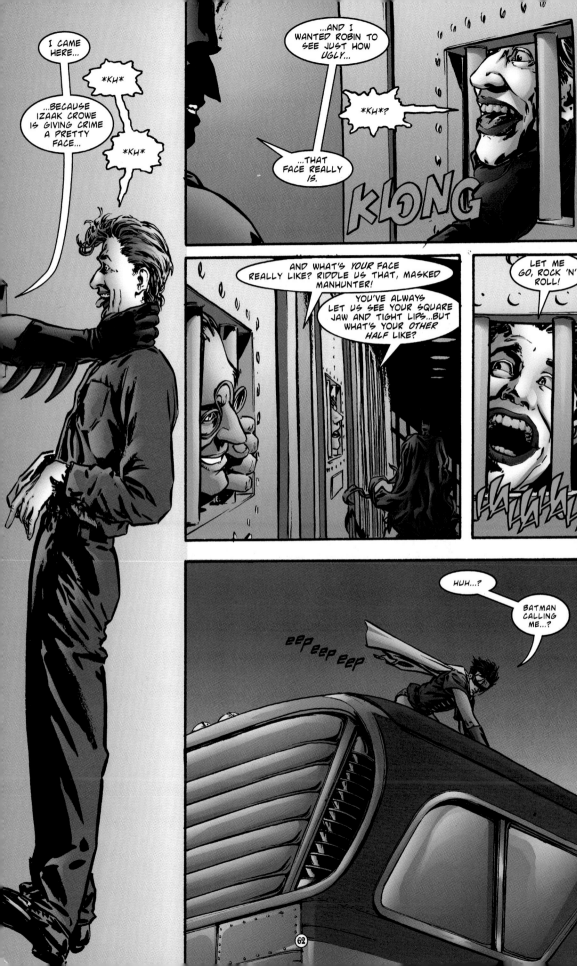

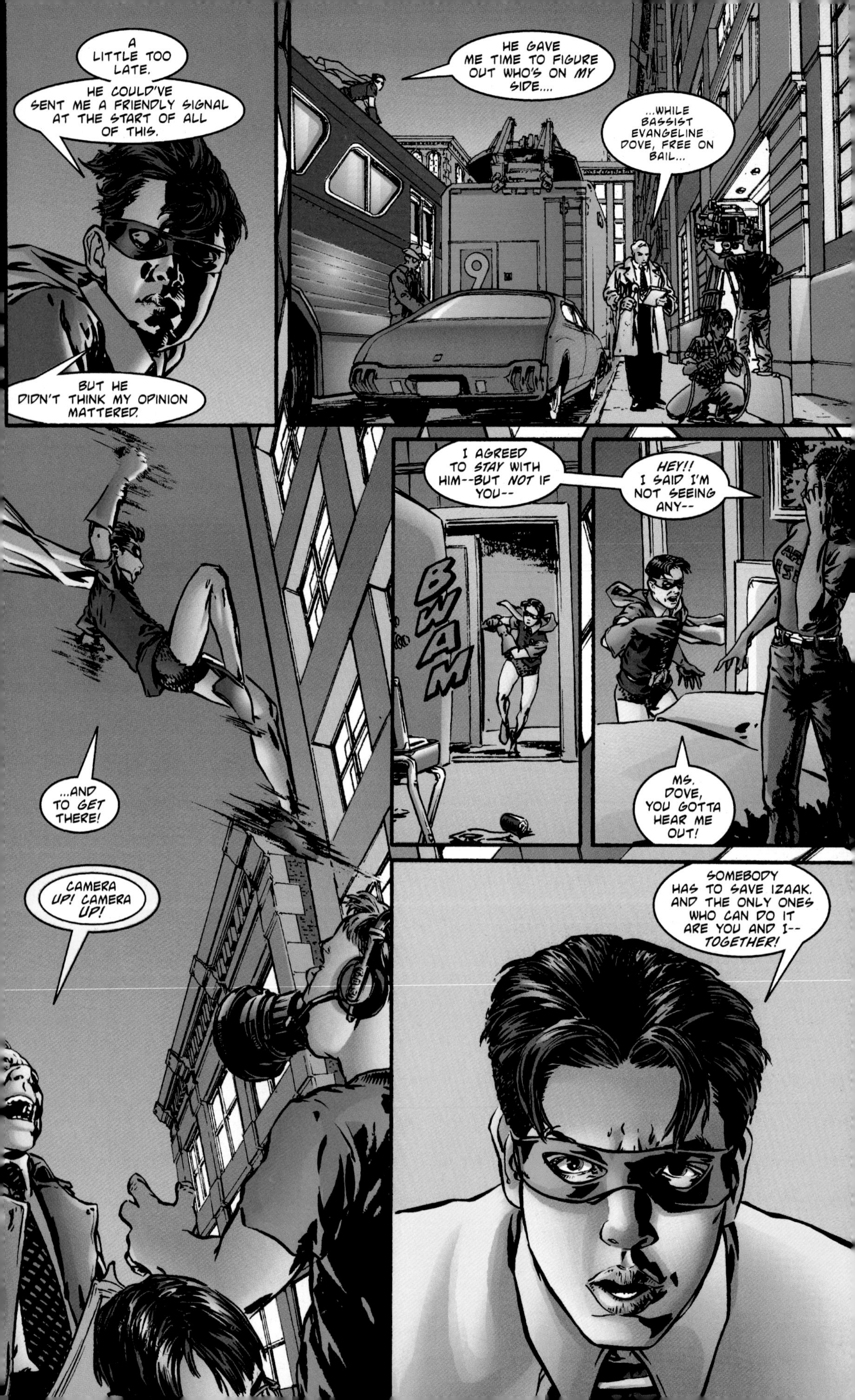
A LITTLE TOO LATE.
HE COULD'VE SENT ME A FRIENDLY SIGNAL AT THE START OF ALL OF THIS.
BUT HE DIDN'T THINK MY OPINION MATTERED.
HE GAVE ME TIME TO FIGURE OUT WHO'S ON *MY* SIDE....
...WHILE BASSIST EVANGELINE DOVE, FREE ON BAIL...
...AND TO GET THERE!
CAMERA *UP!* CAMERA *UP!*
I AGREED TO *STAY* WITH HIM--BUT *NOT* IF YOU--
BWAM
HEY!! I SAID I'M NOT SEEING ANY--
MS. DOVE, YOU GOTTA HEAR ME OUT!
SOMEBODY HAS TO SAVE IZAAK. AND THE ONLY ONES WHO CAN DO IT ARE YOU AND I-- *TOGETHER!*

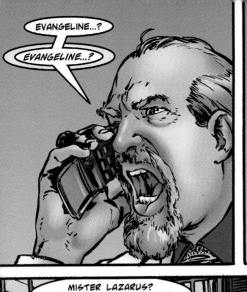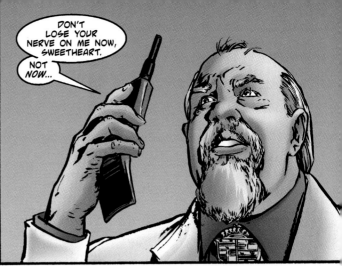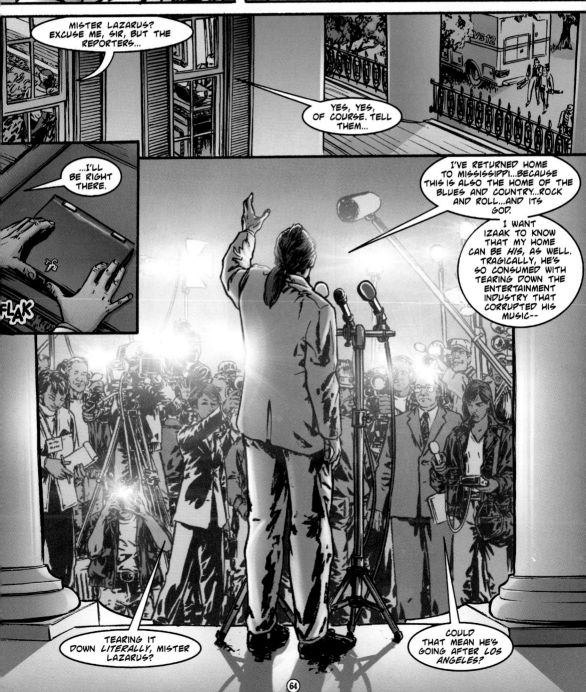

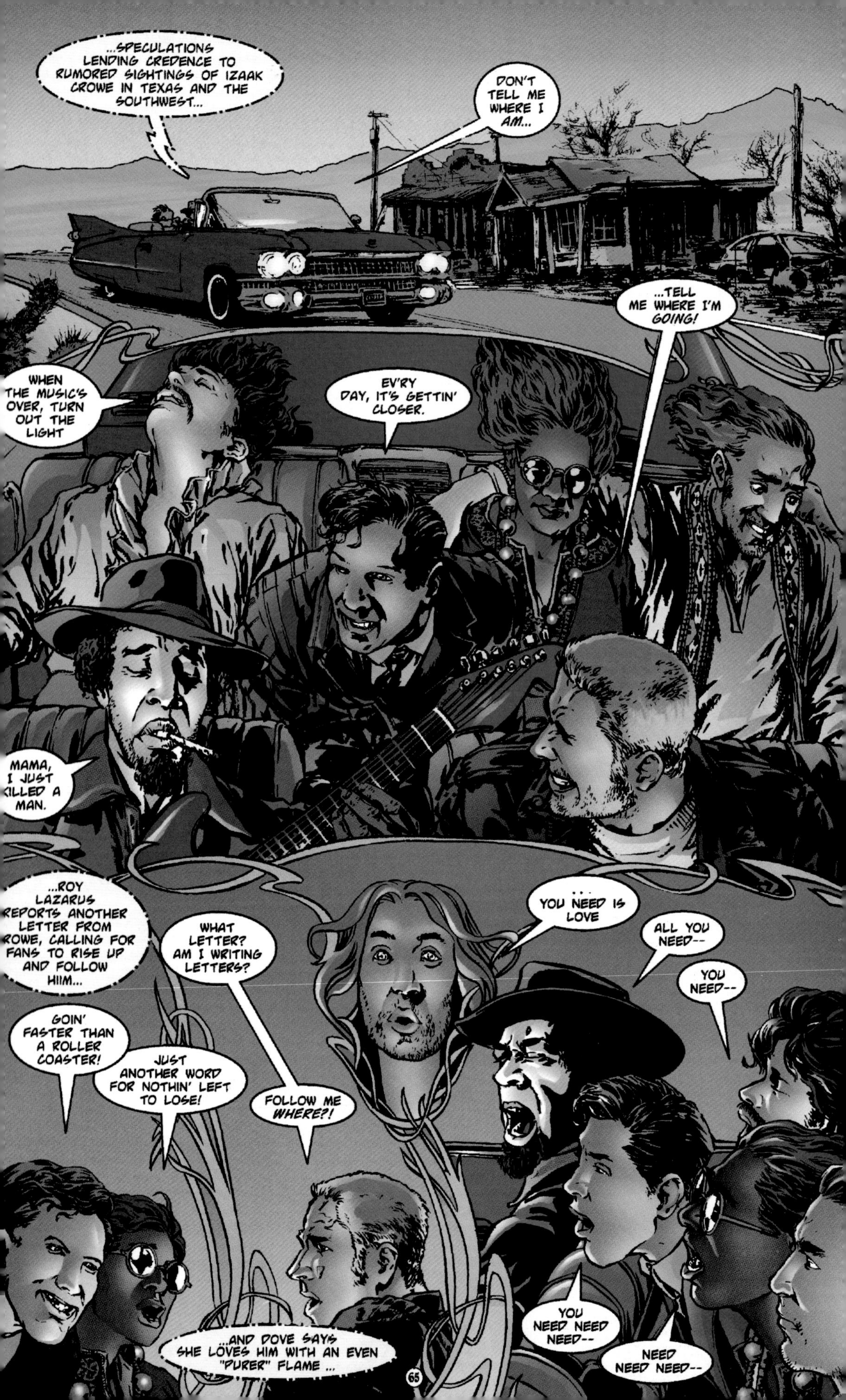

...SPECULATIONS LENDING CREDENCE TO RUMORED SIGHTINGS OF IZAAK CROWE IN TEXAS AND THE SOUTHWEST...
DON'T TELL ME WHERE I AM...
...TELL ME WHERE I'M GOING!
WHEN THE MUSIC'S OVER, TURN OUT THE LIGHT
EV'RY DAY, IT'S GETTIN' CLOSER.
MAMA, I JUST KILLED A MAN.
...ROY LAZARUS REPORTS ANOTHER LETTER FROM CROWE, CALLING FOR FANS TO RISE UP AND FOLLOW HIM...
WHAT LETTER? AM I WRITING LETTERS?
... YOU NEED IS LOVE
ALL YOU NEED--
YOU NEED--
GOIN' FASTER THAN A ROLLER COASTER!
JUST ANOTHER WORD FOR NOTHIN' LEFT TO LOSE!
FOLLOW ME WHERE?!
YOU NEED NEED NEED--
...AND DOVE SAYS SHE LOVES HIM WITH AN EVEN "PURER" FLAME ...
NEED NEED NEED--

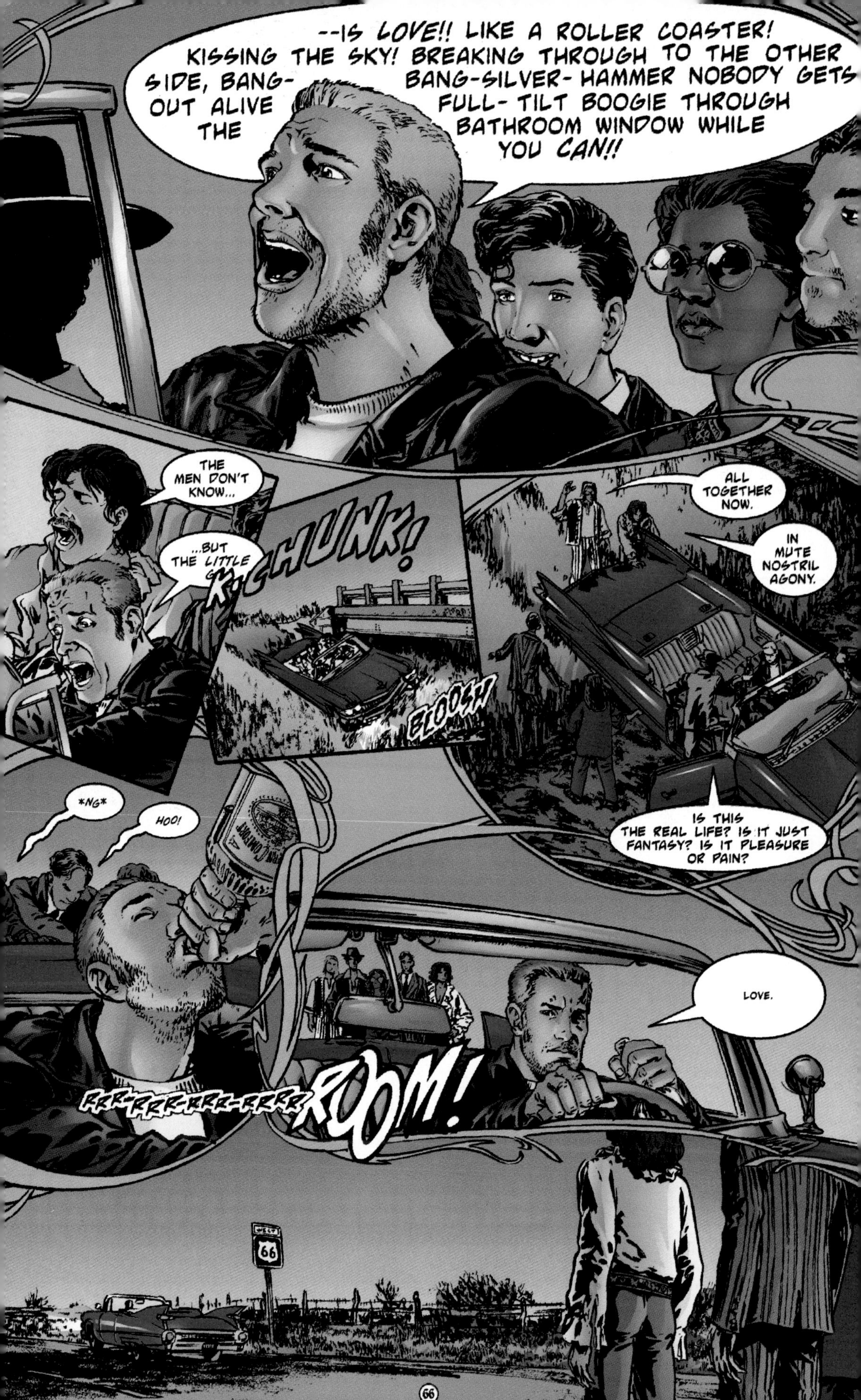

--IS LOVE!! LIKE A ROLLER COASTER! KISSING THE SKY! BREAKING THROUGH TO THE OTHER SIDE, BANG-BANG-SILVER-HAMMER NOBODY GETS OUT ALIVE FULL-TILT BOOGIE THROUGH THE BATHROOM WINDOW WHILE YOU CAN!!
THE MEN DON'T KNOW...
...BUT THE LITTLE G...
K-CHUNK!
BLOOSH
ALL TOGETHER NOW.
IN MUTE NOSTRIL AGONY.
IS THIS THE REAL LIFE? IS IT JUST FANTASY? IS IT PLEASURE OR PAIN?
NG
HOO!
LOVE.
RRR-RRR-RRR-RRRRROOM!
WEST
66

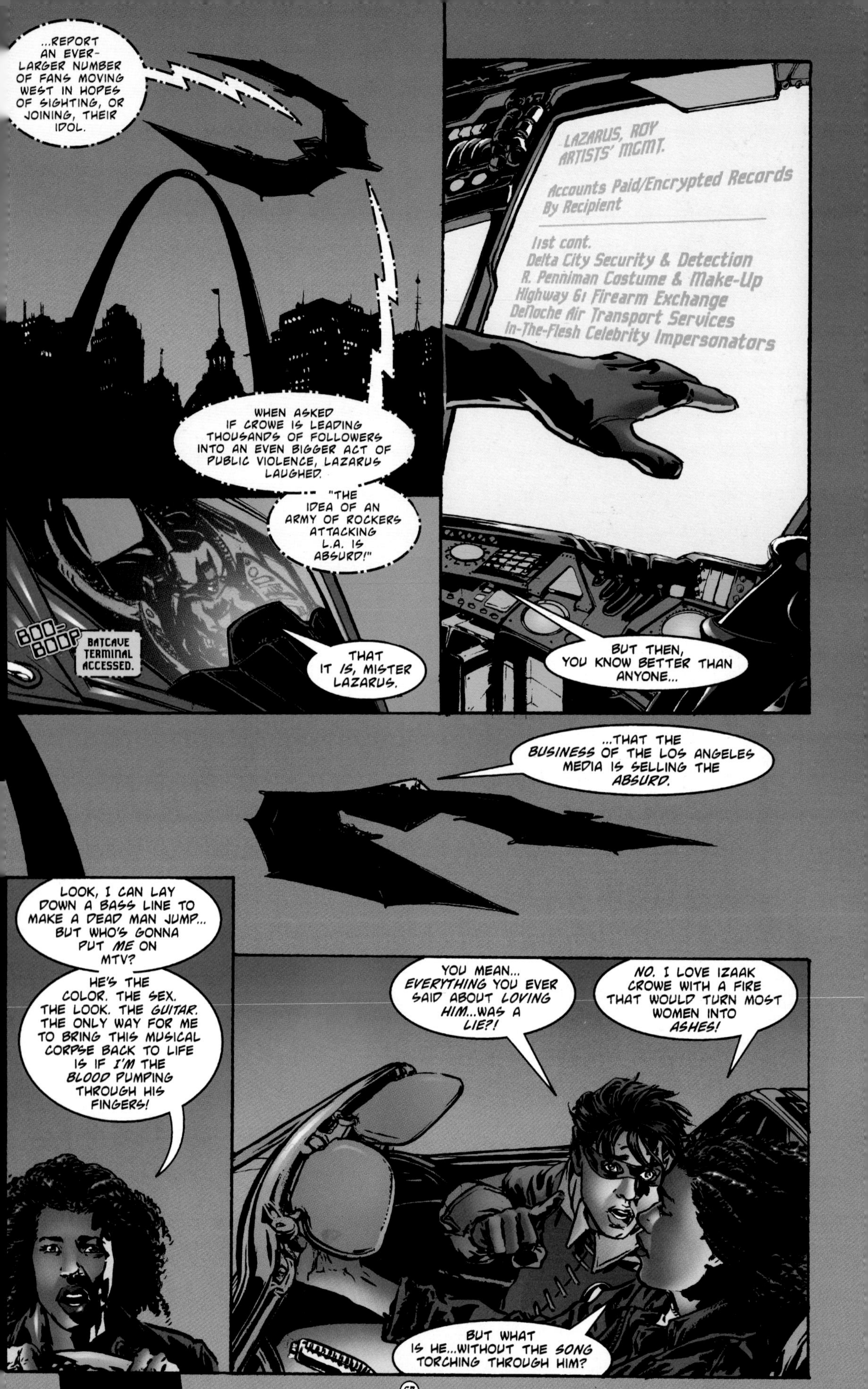
...REPORT AN EVER-LARGER NUMBER OF FANS MOVING WEST IN HOPES OF SIGHTING, OR JOINING, THEIR IDOL.
WHEN ASKED IF CROWE IS LEADING THOUSANDS OF FOLLOWERS INTO AN EVEN BIGGER ACT OF PUBLIC VIOLENCE, LAZARUS LAUGHED.
"THE IDEA OF AN ARMY OF ROCKERS ATTACKING L.A. IS ABSURD!"
BOO-BOOP
BATCAVE TERMINAL ACCESSED.
THAT IT *IS*, MISTER LAZARUS.
LAZARUS, ROY
ARTISTS' MGMT.
Accounts Paid/Encrypted Records By Recipient
1ist cont.
Delta City Security & Detection
R. Penniman Costume & Make-Up
Highway 61 Firearm Exchange
DeNoche Air Transport Services
In-The-Flesh Celebrity Impersonators
BUT THEN, YOU KNOW BETTER THAN ANYONE...
...THAT THE *BUSINESS* OF THE LOS ANGELES MEDIA IS SELLING THE *ABSURD*.
LOOK, I CAN LAY DOWN A BASS LINE TO MAKE A DEAD MAN JUMP... BUT WHO'S GONNA PUT *ME* ON MTV?
HE'S THE COLOR. THE SEX. THE LOOK. THE *GUITAR*. THE ONLY WAY FOR ME TO BRING THIS MUSICAL CORPSE BACK TO LIFE IS IF *I'M* THE *BLOOD PUMPING* THROUGH HIS FINGERS!
YOU MEAN... *EVERYTHING* YOU EVER SAID ABOUT *LOVING HIM*...WAS A *LIE*?!
NO. I LOVE IZAAK CROWE WITH A FIRE THAT WOULD TURN MOST WOMEN INTO *ASHES!*
BUT WHAT IS HE...WITHOUT THE *SONG* TORCHING THROUGH HIM?

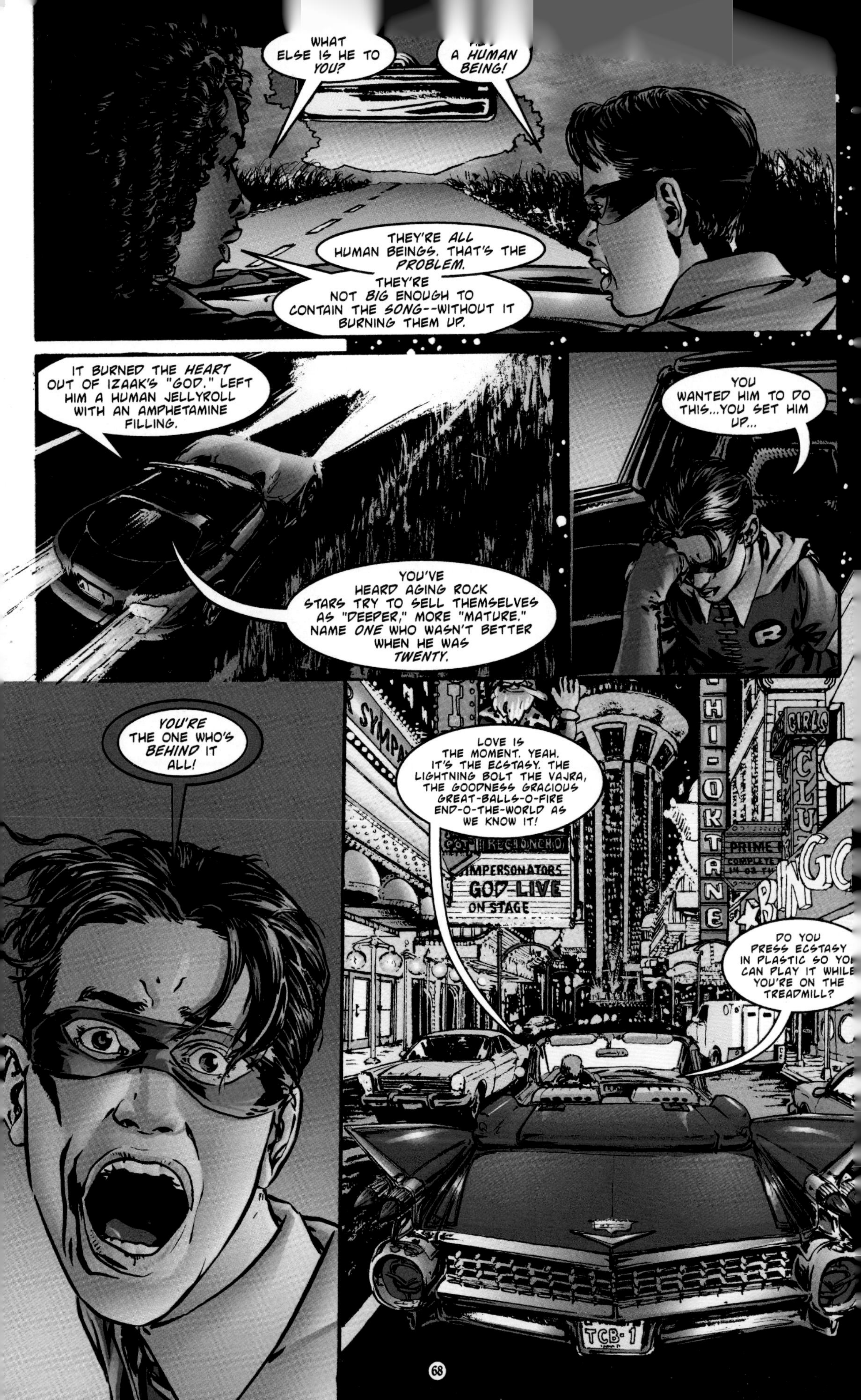
WHAT ELSE IS HE TO YOU?
A HUMAN BEING!
THEY'RE ALL HUMAN BEINGS. THAT'S THE PROBLEM.
THEY'RE NOT BIG ENOUGH TO CONTAIN THE SONG--WITHOUT IT BURNING THEM UP.
IT BURNED THE HEART OUT OF IZAAK'S "GOD." LEFT HIM A HUMAN JELLYROLL WITH AN AMPHETAMINE FILLING.
YOU'VE HEARD AGING ROCK STARS TRY TO SELL THEMSELVES AS "DEEPER," MORE "MATURE." NAME ONE WHO WASN'T BETTER WHEN HE WAS TWENTY.
YOU WANTED HIM TO DO THIS...YOU SET HIM UP...
YOU'RE THE ONE WHO'S BEHIND IT ALL!
LOVE IS THE MOMENT. YEAH. IT'S THE ECSTASY. THE LIGHTNING BOLT THE VAJRA, THE GOODNESS GRACIOUS GREAT-BALLS-O-FIRE END-O-THE-WORLD AS WE KNOW IT!
IMPERSONATORS
GOD-LIVE
ON STAGE
HI-OKTANE
GIRLS
BINGO
DO YOU PRESS ECSTASY IN PLASTIC SO YOU CAN PLAY IT WHILE YOU'RE ON THE TREADMILL?
TCB-1

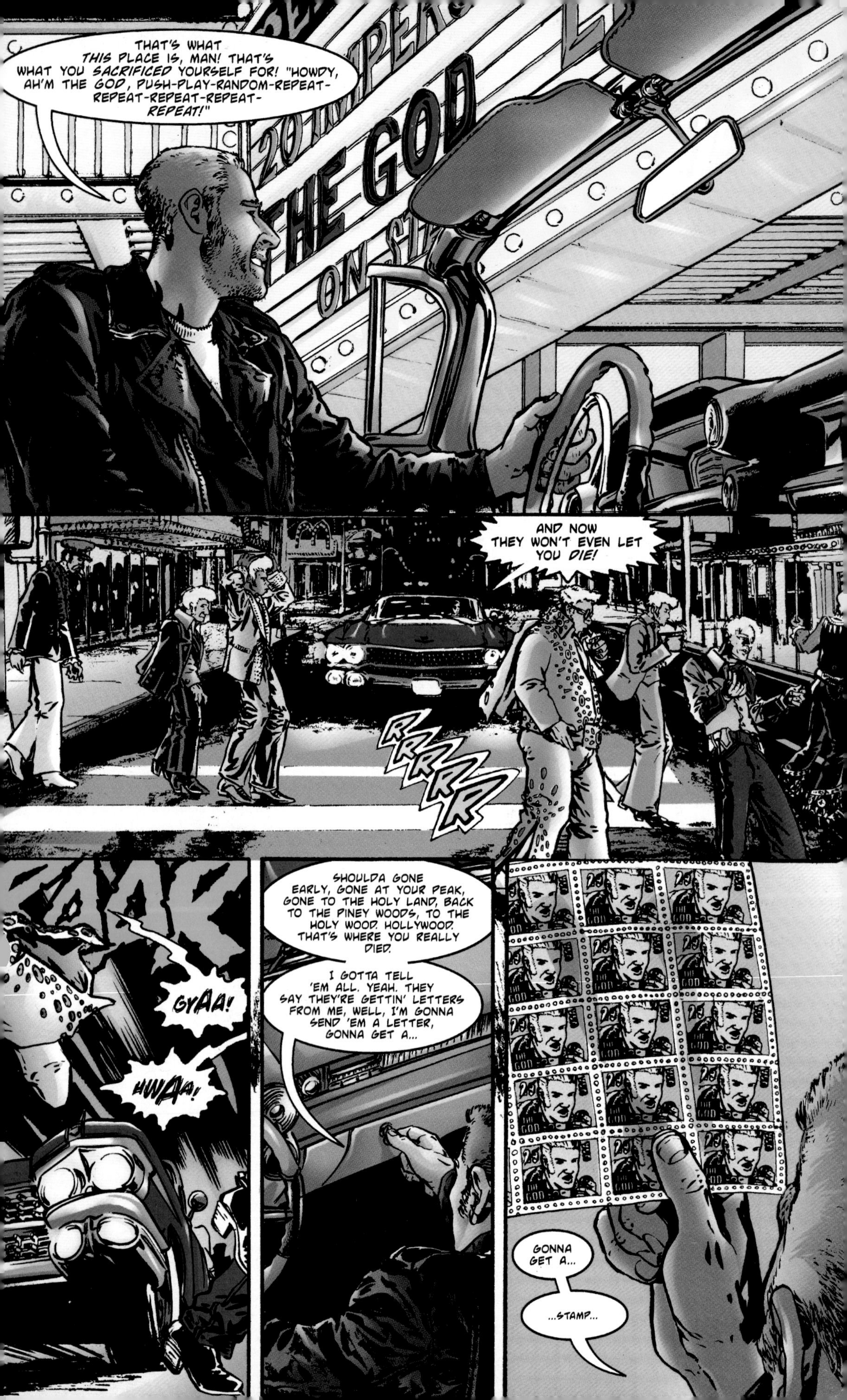
THAT'S WHAT *THIS* PLACE IS, MAN! THAT'S WHAT YOU *SACRIFICED* YOURSELF FOR! "HOWDY, AH'M THE GOD, PUSH-PLAY-RANDOM-REPEAT-REPEAT-REPEAT-REPEAT-REPEAT-*REPEAT!*"
THE GOD
AND NOW THEY WON'T EVEN LET YOU *DIE!*
RRRRR
GYAA!
UWAA!
SHOULDA GONE EARLY, GONE AT YOUR PEAK, GONE TO THE HOLY LAND, BACK TO THE PINEY WOODS, TO THE HOLY WOOD. HOLLYWOOD. THAT'S WHERE YOU REALLY DIED.
I GOTTA TELL 'EM ALL. YEAH. THEY SAY THEY'RE GETTIN' LETTERS FROM ME, WELL, I'M GONNA SEND 'EM A LETTER, GONNA GET A...
GONNA GET A...
...STAMP...

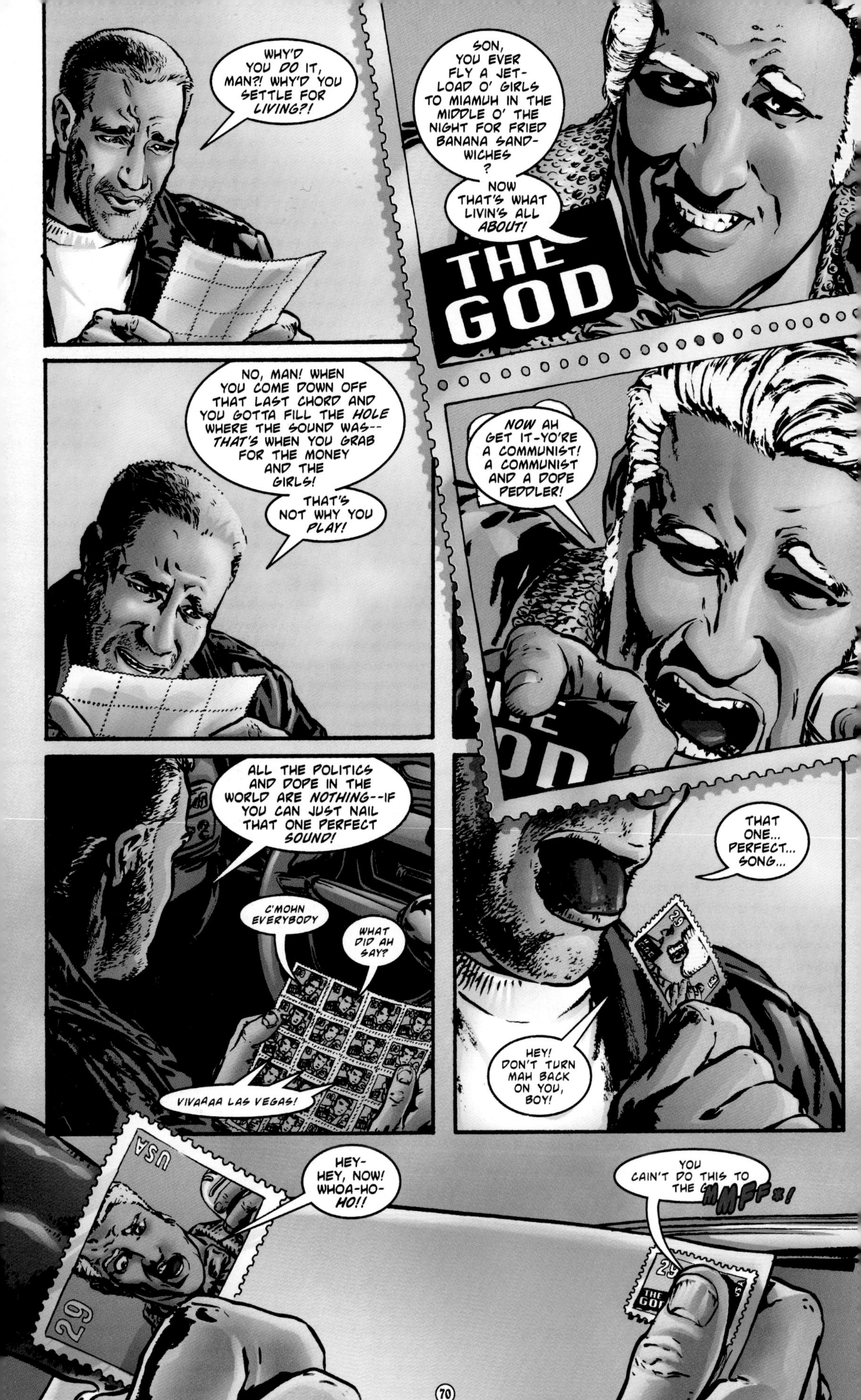
WHY'D YOU DO IT, MAN?! WHY'D YOU SETTLE FOR LIVING?!
SON, YOU EVER FLY A JET-LOAD O' GIRLS TO MIAMUH IN THE MIDDLE O' THE NIGHT FOR FRIED BANANA SAND-WICHES ?
NOW THAT'S WHAT LIVIN'S ALL ABOUT!
THE GOD
NO, MAN! WHEN YOU COME DOWN OFF THAT LAST CHORD AND YOU GOTTA FILL THE HOLE WHERE THE SOUND WAS-- THAT'S WHEN YOU GRAB FOR THE MONEY AND THE GIRLS!
THAT'S NOT WHY YOU PLAY!
NOW AH GET IT-YO'RE A COMMUNIST! A COMMUNIST AND A DOPE PEDDLER!
ALL THE POLITICS AND DOPE IN THE WORLD ARE NOTHING--IF YOU CAN JUST NAIL THAT ONE PERFECT SOUND!
C'MOHN EVERYBODY
WHAT DID AH SAY?
VIVAAAA LAS VEGAS!
THAT ONE... PERFECT... SONG...
HEY! DON'T TURN MAH BACK ON YOU, BOY!
USA
29
HEY-HEY, NOW! WHOA-HO-HO!!
YOU CAIN'T DO THIS TO THE G
MMFF*!

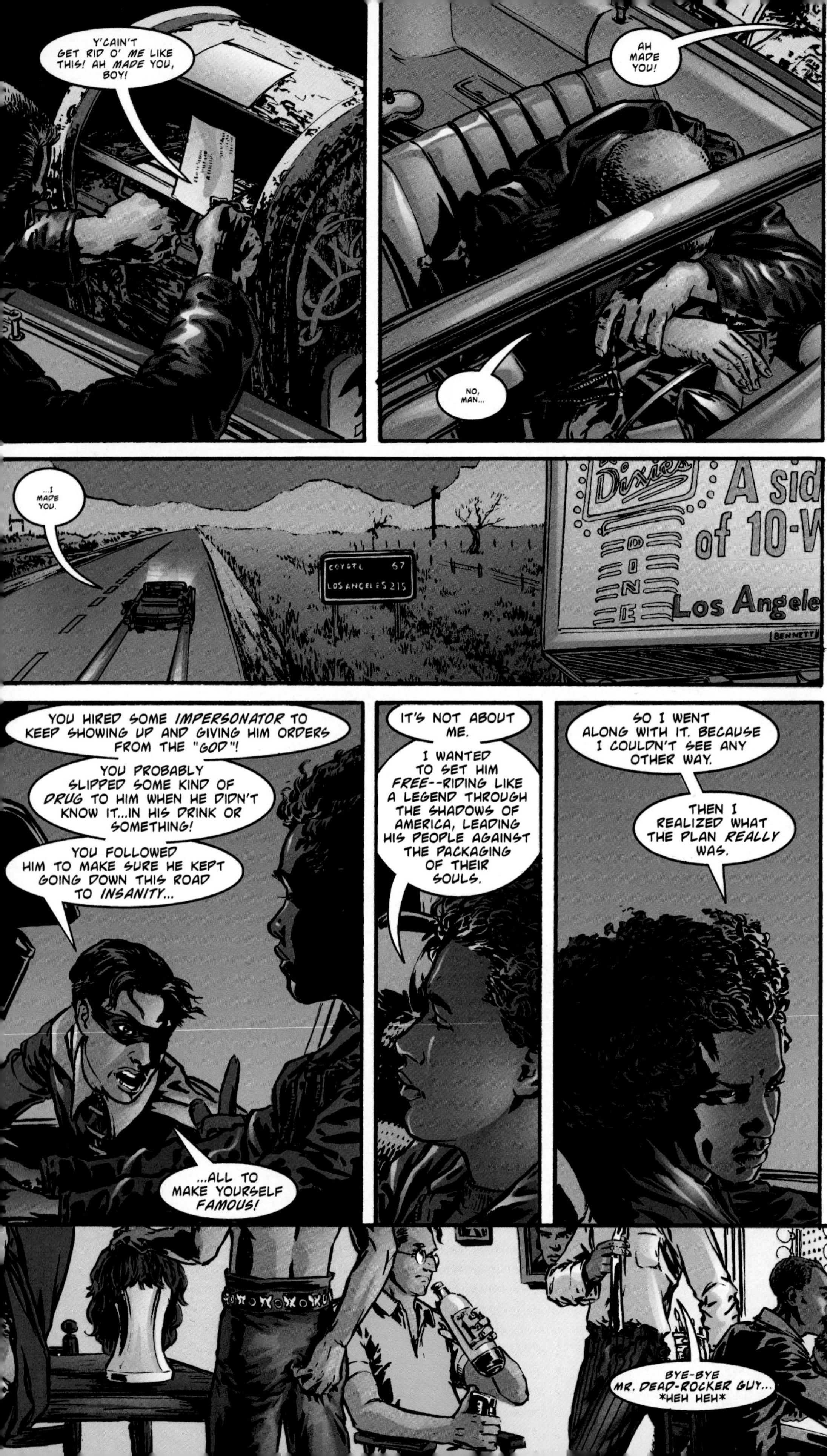

Y'CAIN'T GET RID O' ME LIKE THIS! AH MADE YOU, BOY!
AH MADE YOU!
NO, MAN...
...I MADE YOU.
COYOTL 67
LOS ANGELES 215
Dixie's
DINE
BENNETT
YOU HIRED SOME IMPERSONATOR TO KEEP SHOWING UP AND GIVING HIM ORDERS FROM THE "GOD"!
YOU PROBABLY SLIPPED SOME KIND OF DRUG TO HIM WHEN HE DIDN'T KNOW IT...IN HIS DRINK OR SOMETHING!
YOU FOLLOWED HIM TO MAKE SURE HE KEPT GOING DOWN THIS ROAD TO INSANITY...
...ALL TO MAKE YOURSELF FAMOUS!
IT'S NOT ABOUT ME.
I WANTED TO SET HIM FREE--RIDING LIKE A LEGEND THROUGH THE SHADOWS OF AMERICA, LEADING HIS PEOPLE AGAINST THE PACKAGING OF THEIR SOULS.
SO I WENT ALONG WITH IT. BECAUSE I COULDN'T SEE ANY OTHER WAY.
THEN I REALIZED WHAT THE PLAN REALLY WAS.
BYE-BYE MR. DEAD-ROCKER GUY... *HEH HEH*

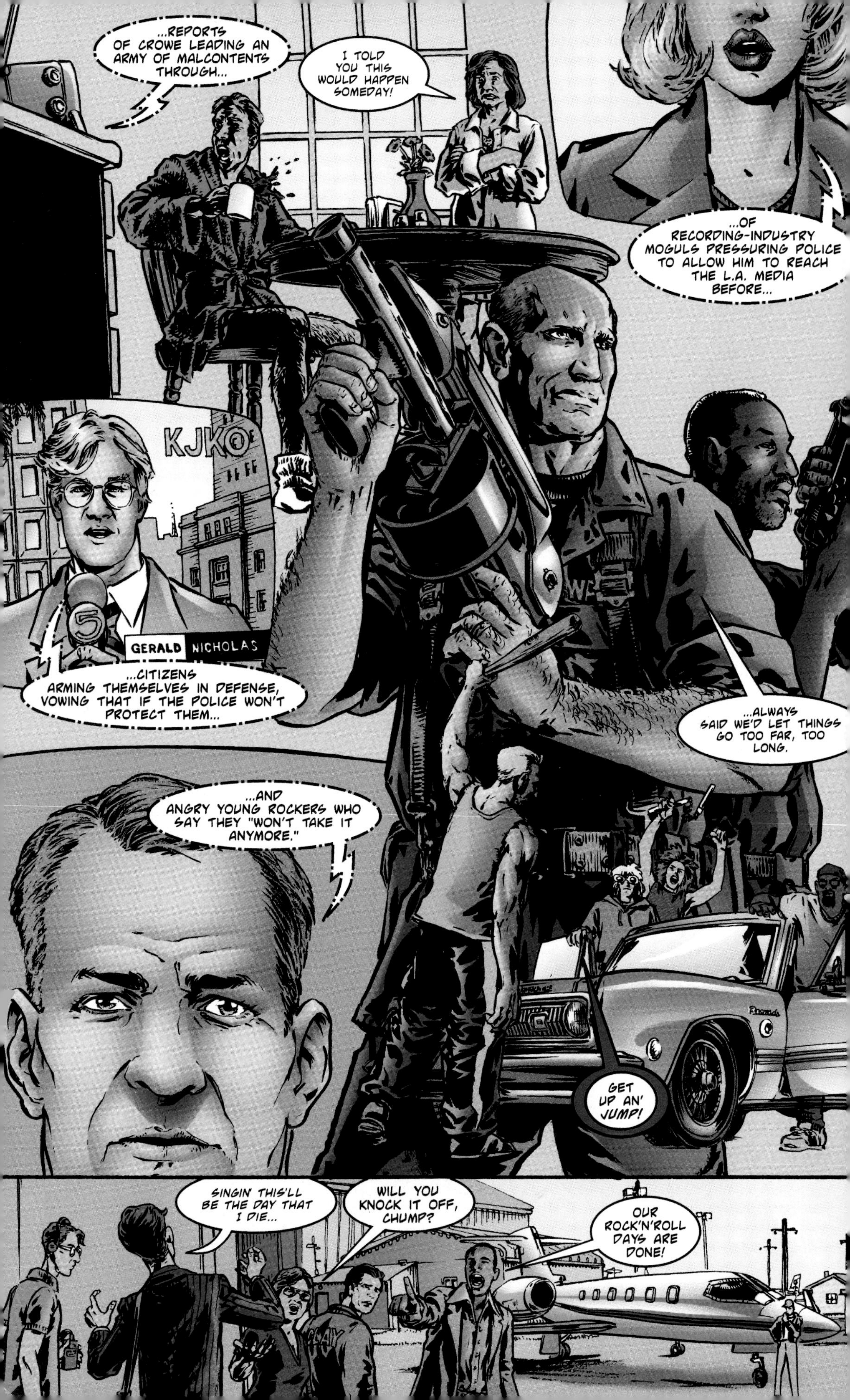
...REPORTS OF CROWE LEADING AN ARMY OF MALCONTENTS THROUGH...
I TOLD YOU THIS WOULD HAPPEN SOMEDAY!
...OF RECORDING-INDUSTRY MOGULS PRESSURING POLICE TO ALLOW HIM TO REACH THE L.A. MEDIA BEFORE...
KJKO
GERALD NICHOLAS
...CITIZENS ARMING THEMSELVES IN DEFENSE, VOWING THAT IF THE POLICE WON'T PROTECT THEM...
...ALWAYS SAID WE'D LET THINGS GO TOO FAR, TOO LONG.
...AND ANGRY YOUNG ROCKERS WHO SAY THEY "WON'T TAKE IT ANYMORE."
GET UP AN' JUMP!
SINGIN' THIS'LL BE THE DAY THAT I DIE...
WILL YOU KNOCK IT OFF, CHUMP?
OUR ROCK'N'ROLL DAYS ARE DONE!

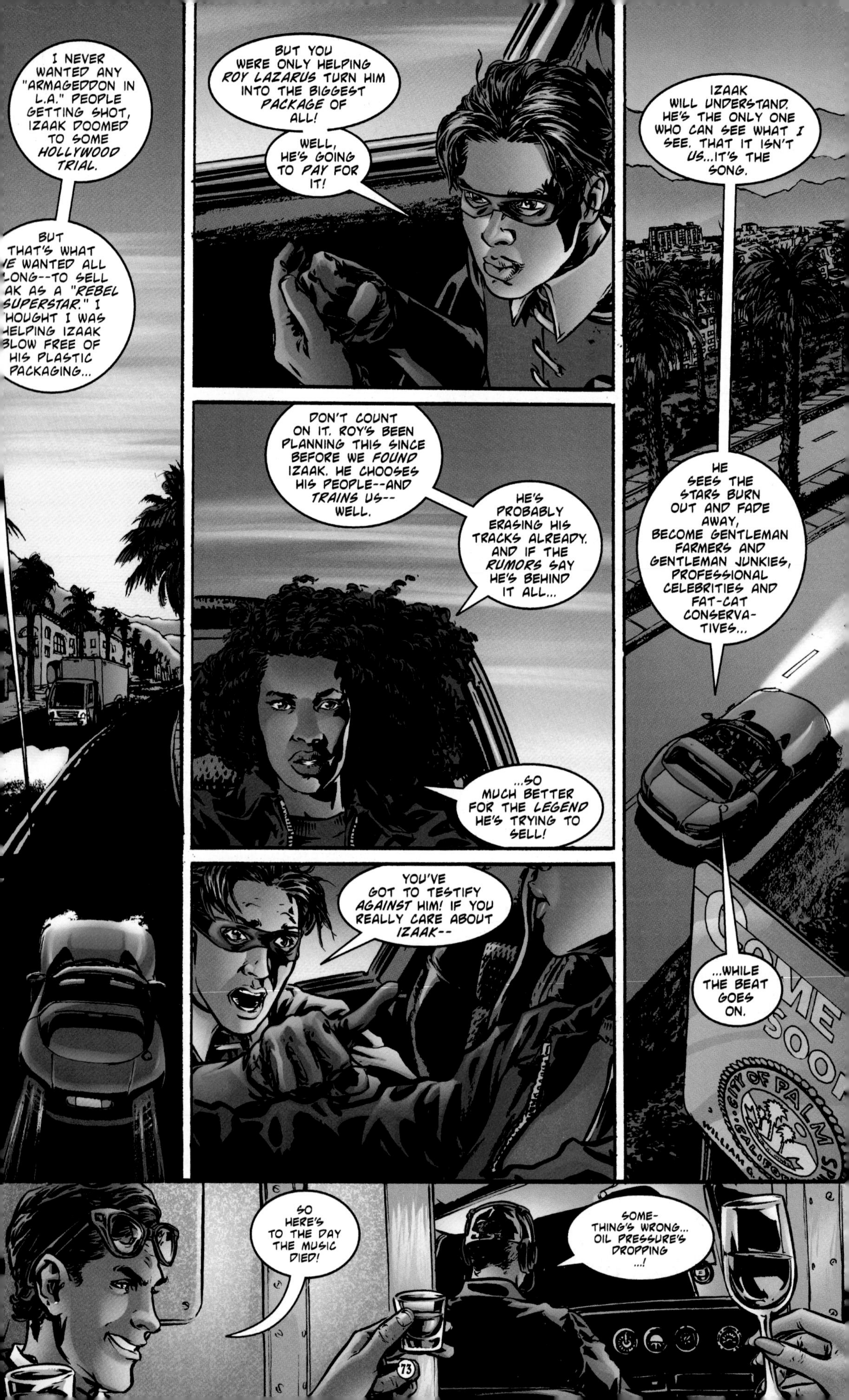
I NEVER WANTED ANY "ARMAGEDDON IN L.A." PEOPLE GETTING SHOT, IZAAK DOOMED TO SOME HOLLYWOOD TRIAL.
BUT THAT'S WHAT E WANTED ALL ONG--TO SELL AK AS A "REBEL SUPERSTAR." I HOUGHT I WAS ELPING IZAAK LOW FREE OF HIS PLASTIC PACKAGING...
BUT YOU WERE ONLY HELPING ROY LAZARUS TURN HIM INTO THE BIGGEST PACKAGE OF ALL!
WELL, HE'S GOING TO PAY FOR IT!
DON'T COUNT ON IT. ROY'S BEEN PLANNING THIS SINCE BEFORE WE FOUND IZAAK. HE CHOOSES HIS PEOPLE--AND TRAINS US--WELL.
HE'S PROBABLY ERASING HIS TRACKS ALREADY. AND IF THE RUMORS SAY HE'S BEHIND IT ALL...
...SO MUCH BETTER FOR THE LEGEND HE'S TRYING TO SELL!
YOU'VE GOT TO TESTIFY AGAINST HIM! IF YOU REALLY CARE ABOUT IZAAK--
IZAAK WILL UNDERSTAND. HE'S THE ONLY ONE WHO CAN SEE WHAT I SEE. THAT IT ISN'T US...IT'S THE SONG.
HE SEES THE STARS BURN OUT AND FADE AWAY, BECOME GENTLEMAN FARMERS AND GENTLEMAN JUNKIES, PROFESSIONAL CELEBRITIES AND FAT-CAT CONSERVA-TIVES...
...WHILE THE BEAT GOES ON.
SO HERE'S TO THE DAY THE MUSIC DIED!
SOME-THING'S WRONG... OIL PRESSURE'S DROPPING ...!

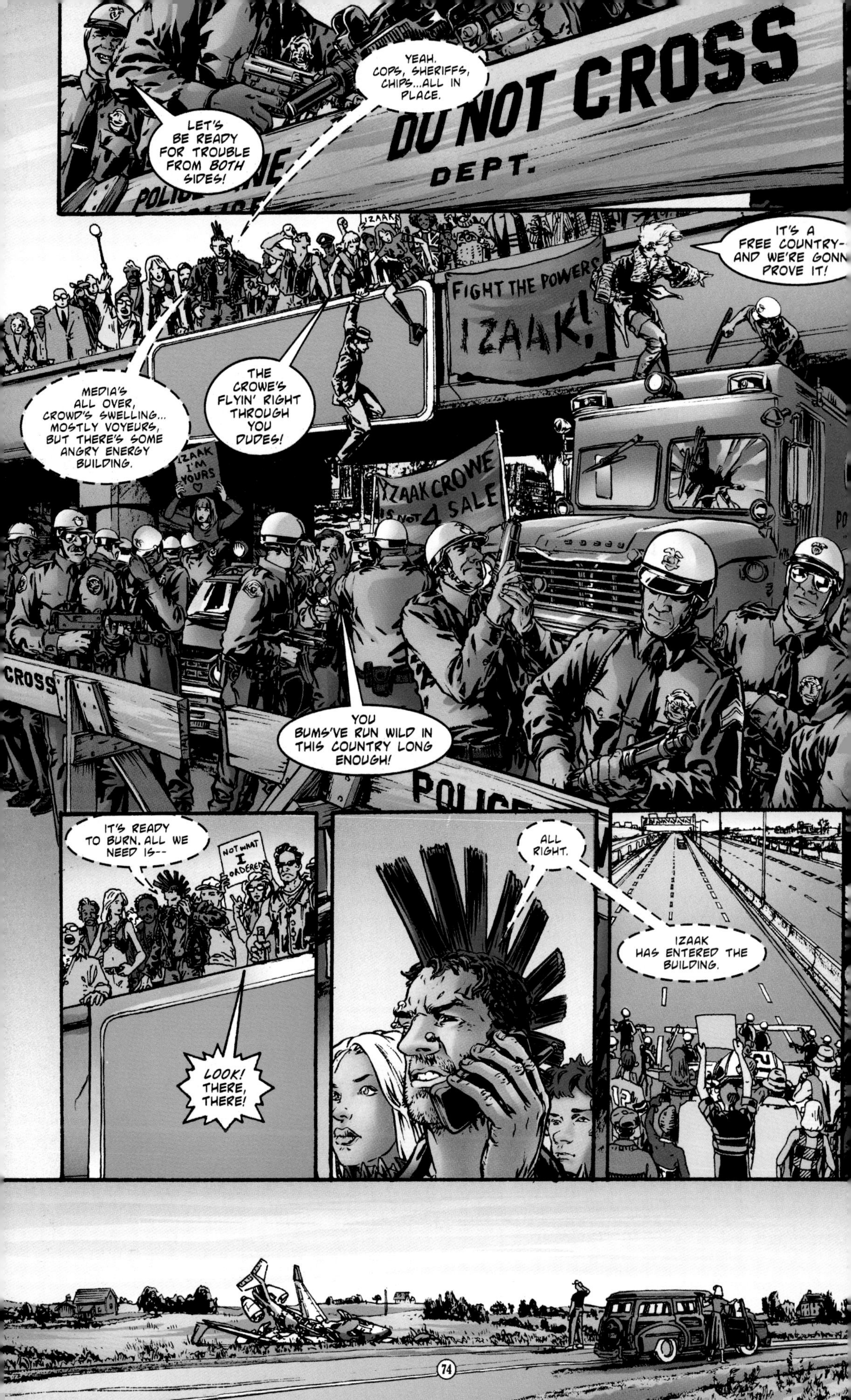
DO NOT CROSS
DEPT.
LET'S BE READY FOR TROUBLE FROM BOTH SIDES!
YEAH. COPS, SHERIFFS, CHIPS...ALL IN PLACE.
FIGHT THE POWERS
IZAAK!
MEDIA'S ALL OVER, CROWD'S SWELLING... MOSTLY VOYEURS, BUT THERE'S SOME ANGRY ENERGY BUILDING.
IZAAK I'M YOURS
THE CROWE'S FLYIN' RIGHT THROUGH YOU DUDES!
IT'S A FREE COUNTRY- AND WE'RE GONN PROVE IT!
IZAAK CROWE IS NOT 4 SALE
CROSS
YOU BUMS'VE RUN WILD IN THIS COUNTRY LONG ENOUGH!
POLICE
IT'S READY TO BURN. ALL WE NEED IS--
NOT WHAT I ORDERED
LOOK! THERE, THERE!
ALL RIGHT.
IZAAK HAS ENTERED THE BUILDING.

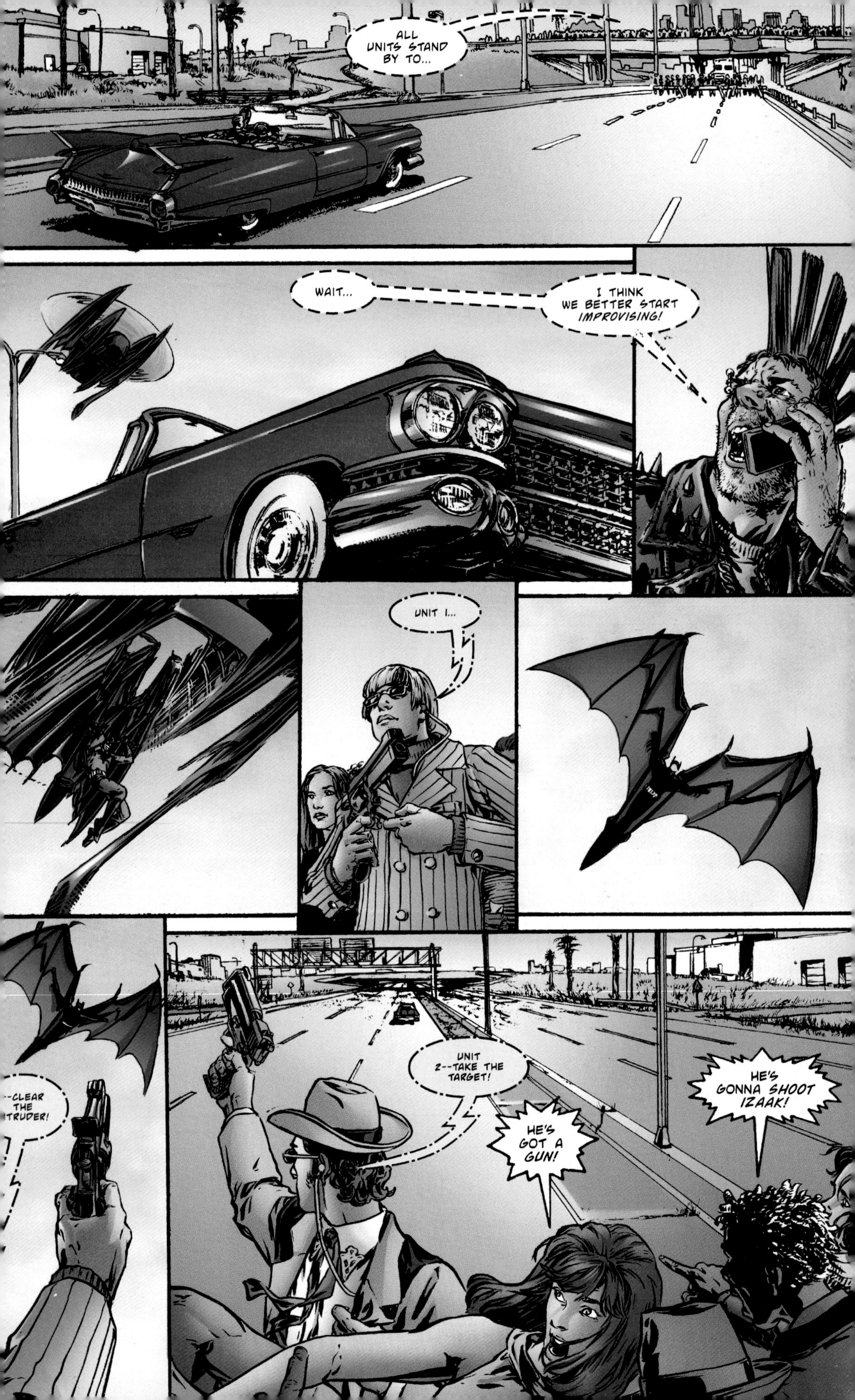
ALL UNITS STAND BY TO...
WAIT...
I THINK WE BETTER START IMPROVISING!
UNIT 1...
--CLEAR THE TRUDER!
UNIT 2--TAKE THE TARGET!
HE'S GOT A GUN!
HE'S GONNA SHOOT IZAAK!

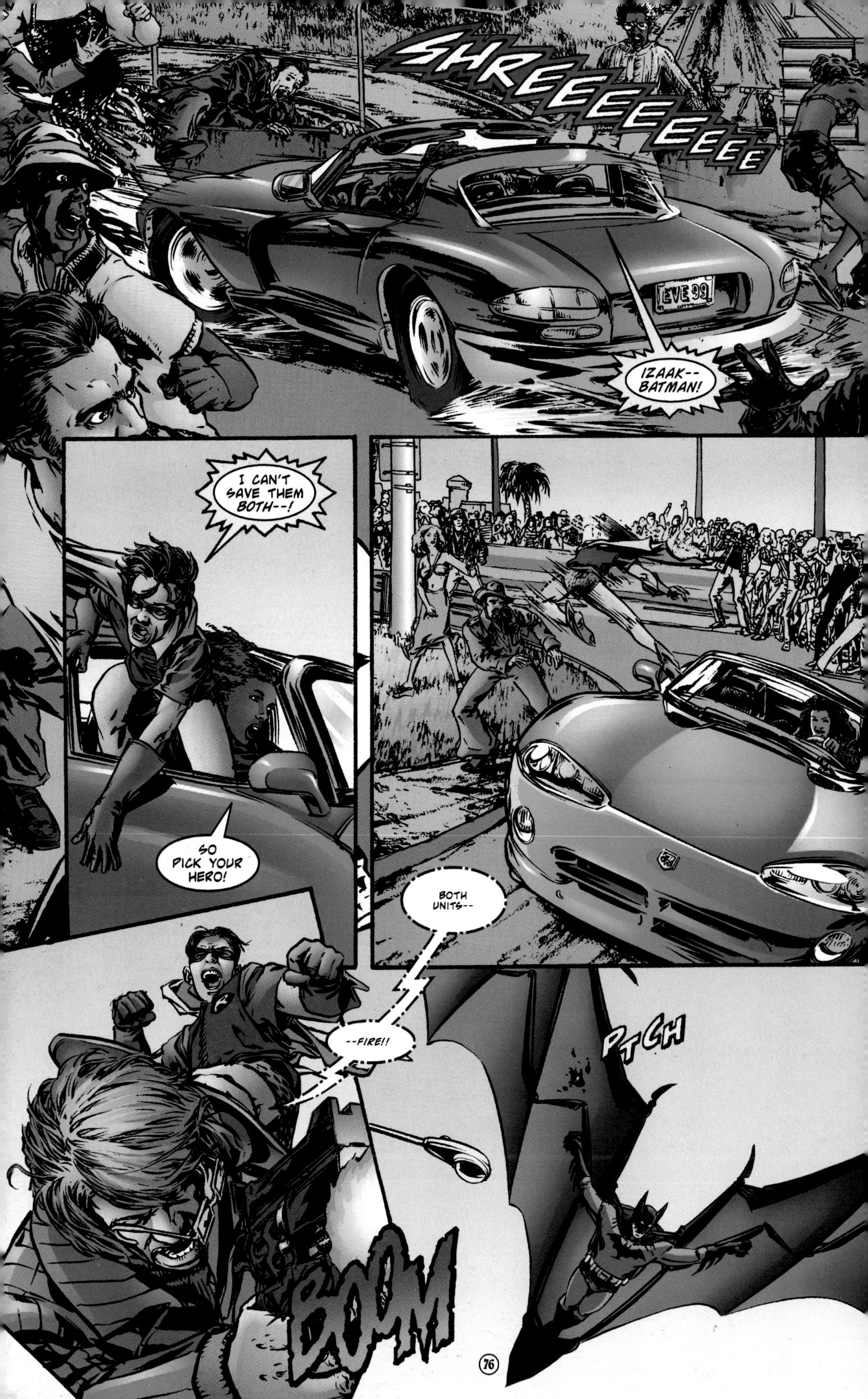

SHREEEEEEEEEE
EVE 99
IZAAK-- BATMAN!
I CAN'T SAVE THEM BOTH--!
SO PICK YOUR HERO!
BOTH UNITS--
--FIRE!!
PTCH
BOOM

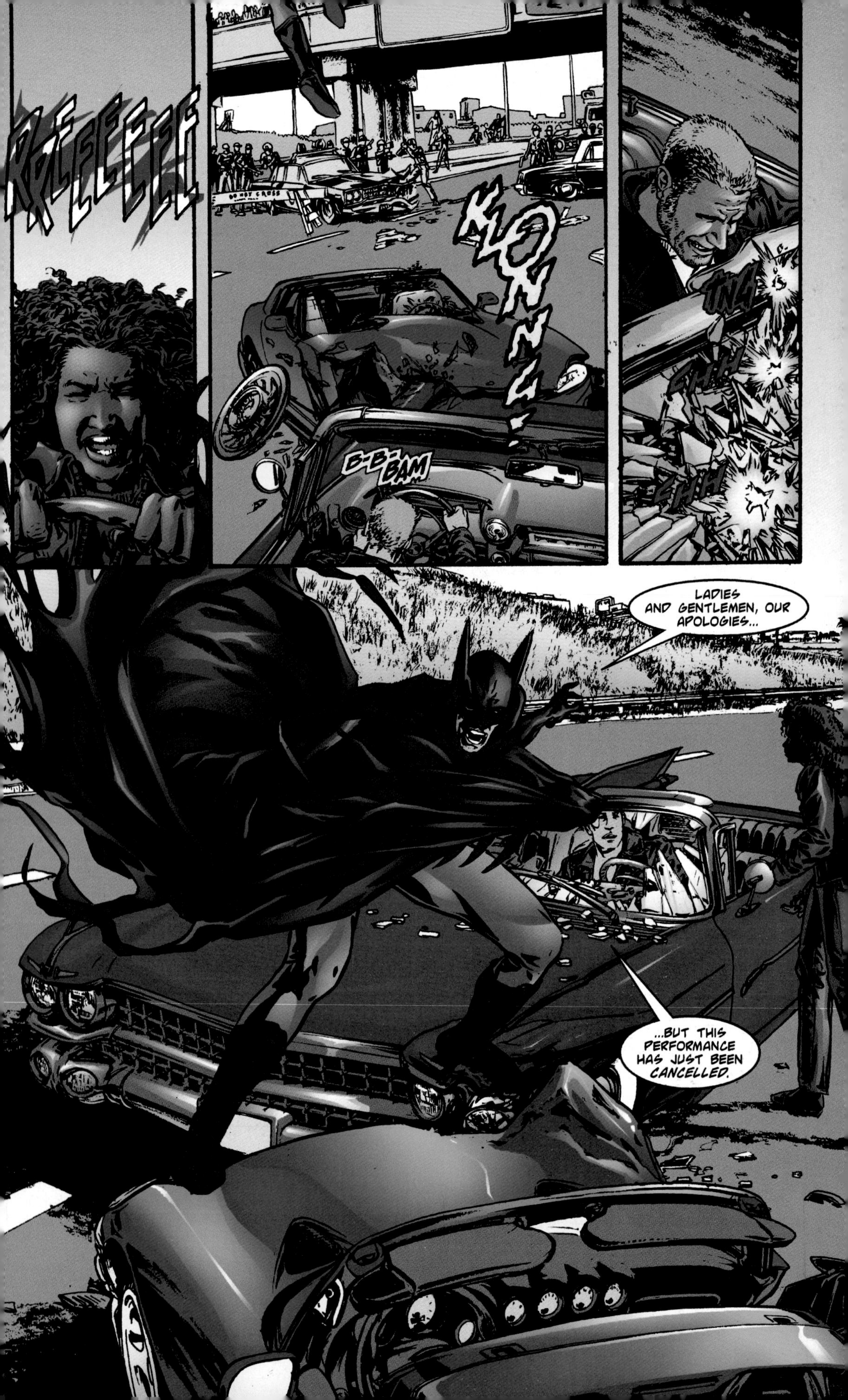
REEEEE
KOWWW!
B-B-BAM
LADIES AND GENTLEMEN, OUR APOLOGIES...
...BUT THIS PERFORMANCE HAS JUST BEEN *CANCELLED*.

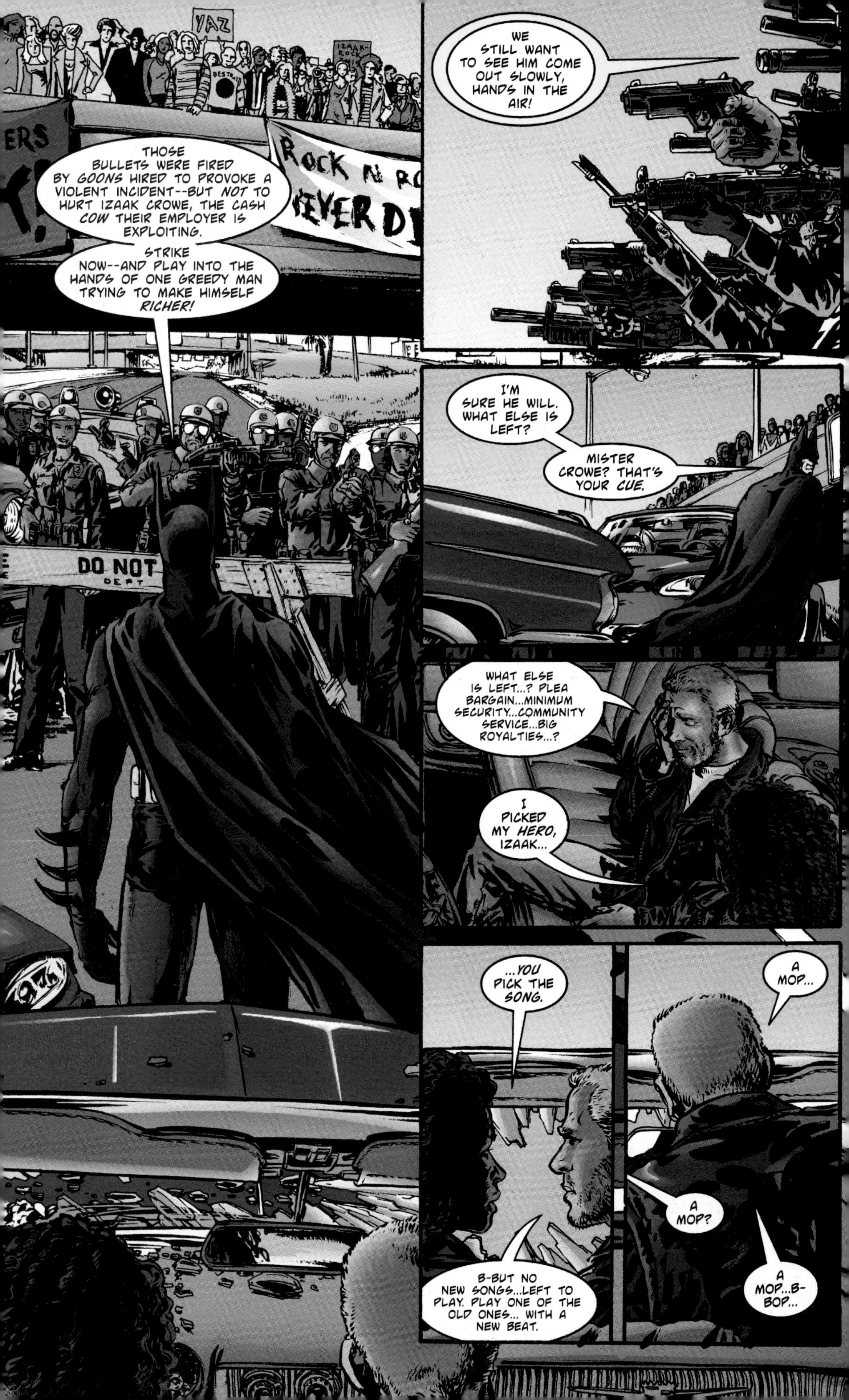
YAZ
THOSE BULLETS WERE FIRED BY *GOONS* HIRED TO PROVOKE A VIOLENT INCIDENT--BUT *NOT* TO HURT IZAAK CROWE, THE CASH *COW* THEIR EMPLOYER IS EXPLOITING.
STRIKE NOW--AND PLAY INTO THE HANDS OF ONE GREEDY MAN TRYING TO MAKE HIMSELF *RICHER!*
DO NOT
WE STILL WANT TO SEE HIM COME OUT SLOWLY, HANDS IN THE AIR!
I'M SURE HE WILL. WHAT ELSE IS LEFT?
MISTER CROWE? THAT'S YOUR *CUE.*
WHAT ELSE IS LEFT...? PLEA BARGAIN...MINIMUM SECURITY...COMMUNITY SERVICE...BIG ROYALTIES...?
I PICKED MY *HERO,* IZAAK...
...*YOU* PICK THE SONG.
B-BUT NO NEW SONGS...LEFT TO PLAY. PLAY ONE OF THE OLD ONES... WITH A NEW BEAT.
A MOP...
A MOP?
A MOP...B-BOP...

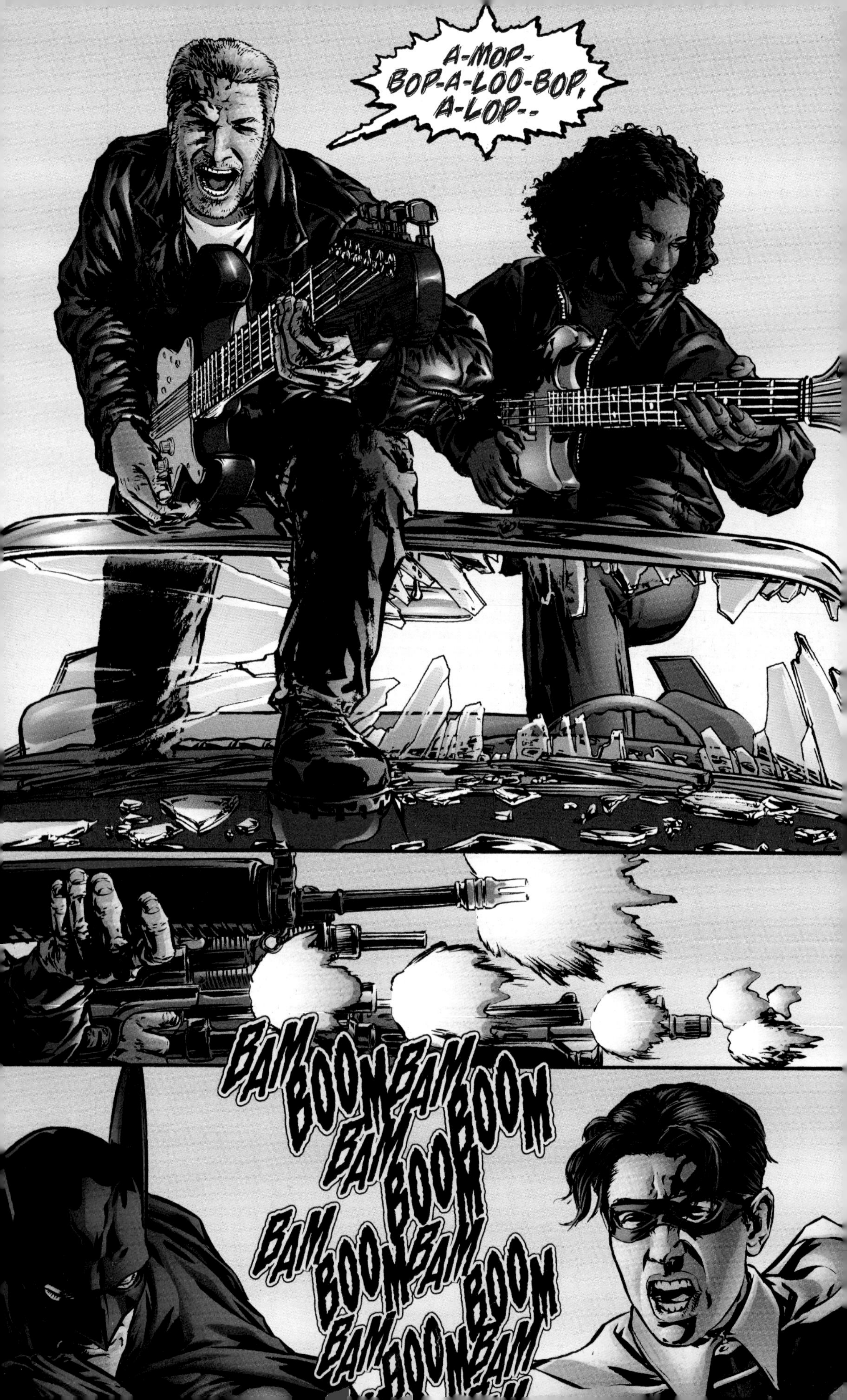
A-MOP-BOP-A-LOO-BOP, A-LOP--
BAM BOOM BAM BOOM
BAM BOOM
BAM BOOM BAM BOOM
BAM BOOM BAM

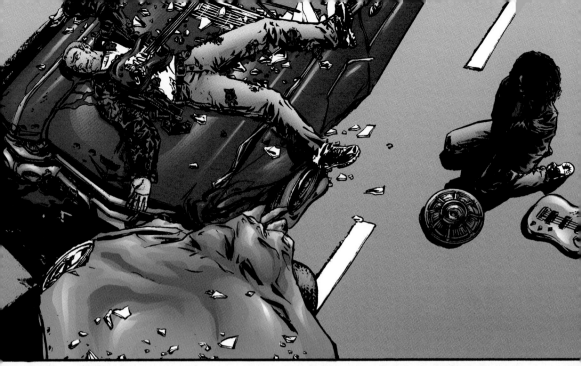

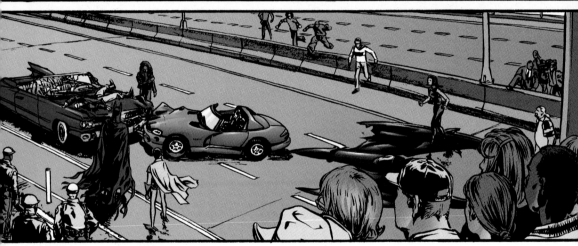

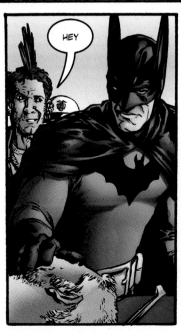

HEY

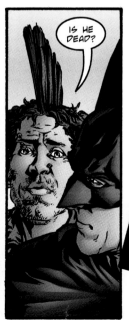

IS HE DEAD?

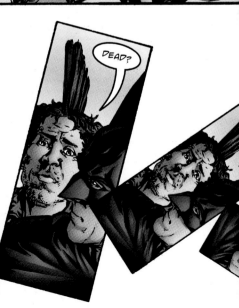

DEAD?

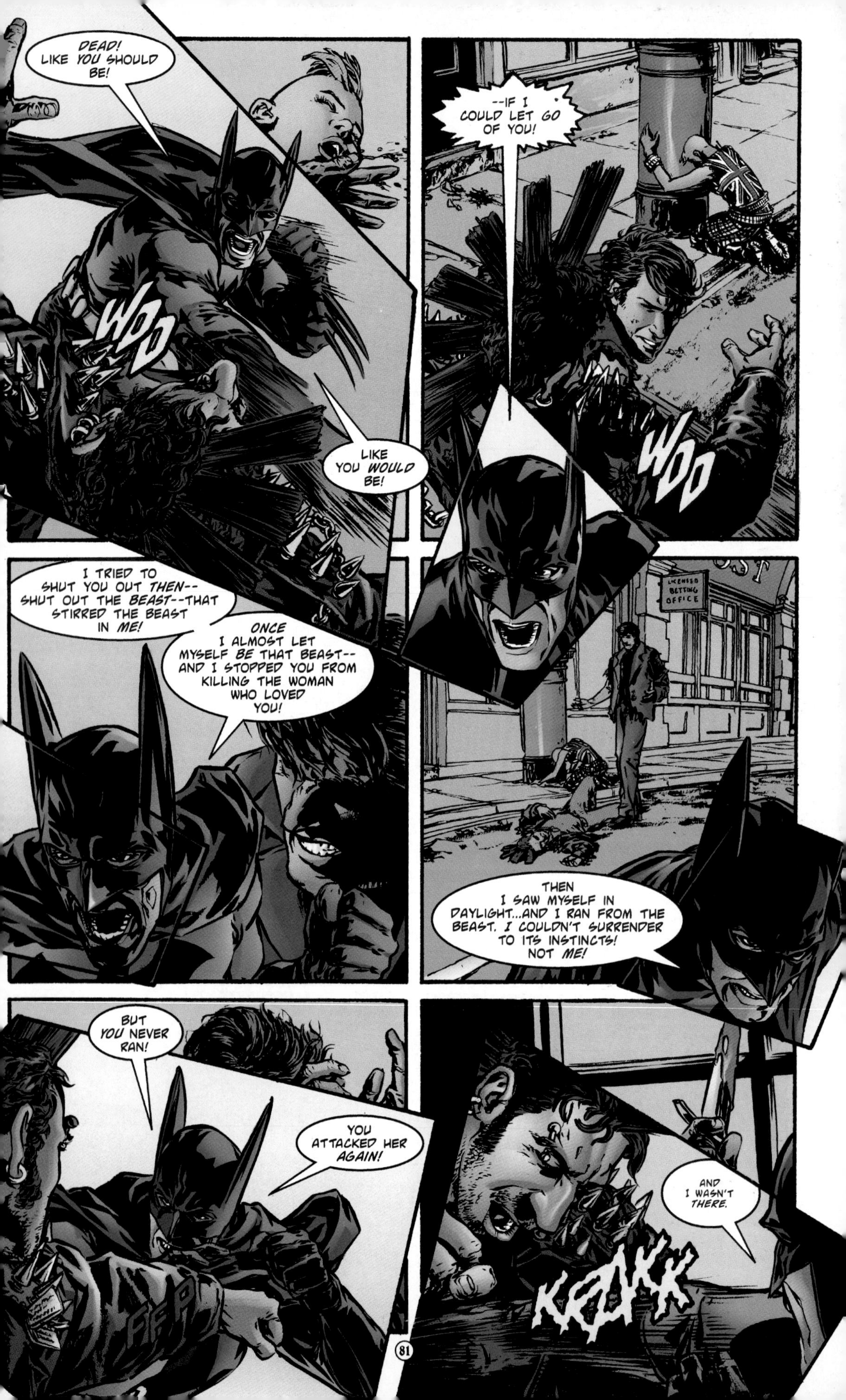
DEAD! LIKE YOU SHOULD BE!
WOO
LIKE YOU WOULD BE!
--IF I COULD LET GO OF YOU!
WOO
I TRIED TO SHUT YOU OUT THEN-- SHUT OUT THE BEAST--THAT STIRRED THE BEAST IN ME!
ONCE I ALMOST LET MYSELF BE THAT BEAST-- AND I STOPPED YOU FROM KILLING THE WOMAN WHO LOVED YOU!
LICENSED BETTING OFFICE
THEN I SAW MYSELF IN DAYLIGHT...AND I RAN FROM THE BEAST. I COULDN'T SURRENDER TO ITS INSTINCTS! NOT ME!
BUT YOU NEVER RAN!
YOU ATTACKED HER AGAIN!
AND I WASN'T THERE.
KRAKK

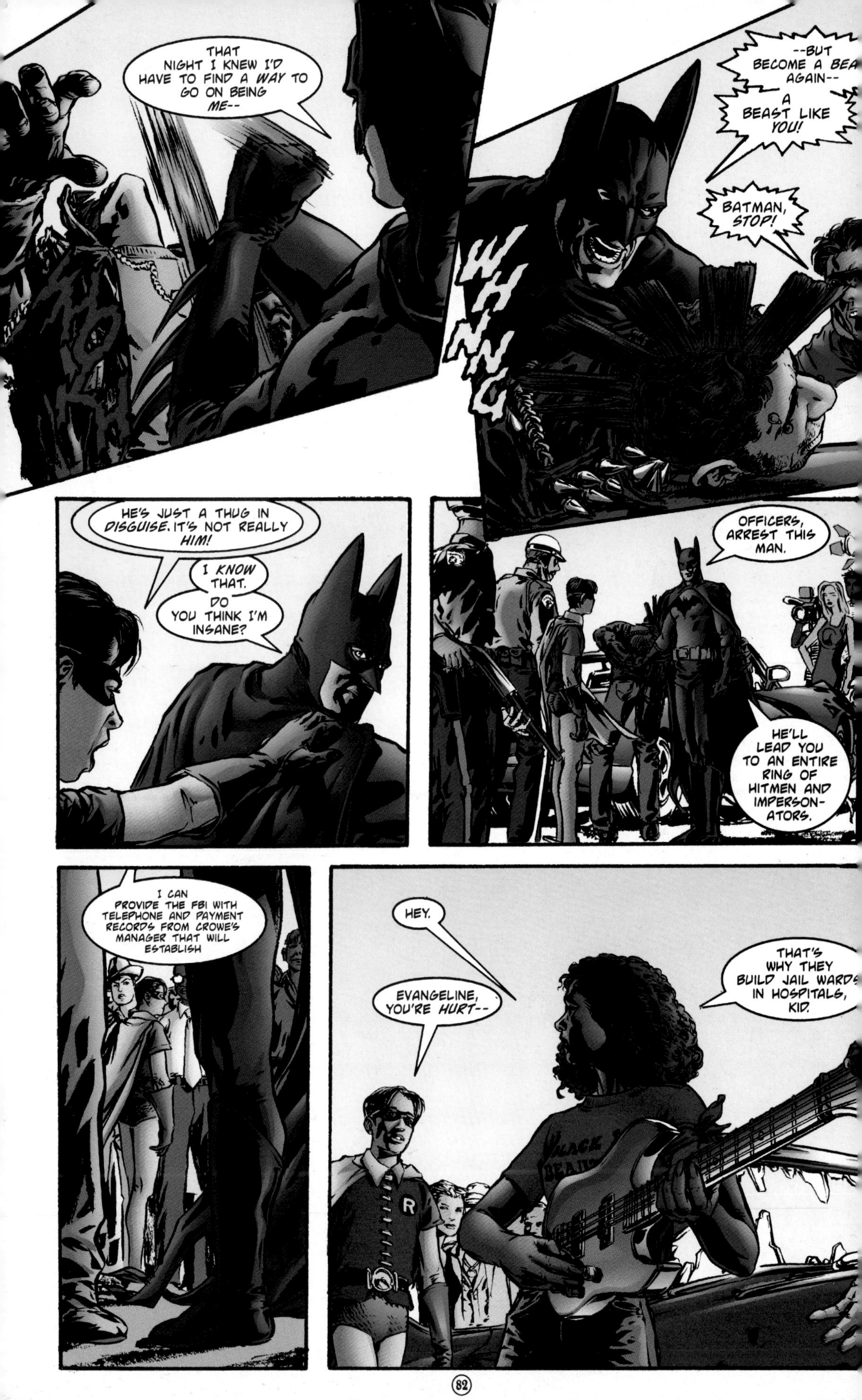
THAT NIGHT I KNEW I'D HAVE TO FIND A *WAY* TO GO ON BEING *ME*--
--BUT BECOME A BEA AGAIN--
A BEAST LIKE *YOU!*
BATMAN, *STOP!*
WHNG
HE'S JUST A THUG IN *DISGUISE*. IT'S NOT REALLY *HIM!*
I *KNOW* THAT.
DO YOU THINK I'M INSANE?
OFFICERS, ARREST THIS MAN.
HE'LL LEAD YOU TO AN ENTIRE RING OF HITMEN AND IMPERSON-ATORS.
I CAN PROVIDE THE FBI WITH TELEPHONE AND PAYMENT RECORDS FROM CROWE'S MANAGER THAT WILL ESTABLISH
HEY.
EVANGELINE, YOU'RE *HURT*--
THAT'S WHY THEY BUILD JAIL WARDS IN HOSPITALS, KID.

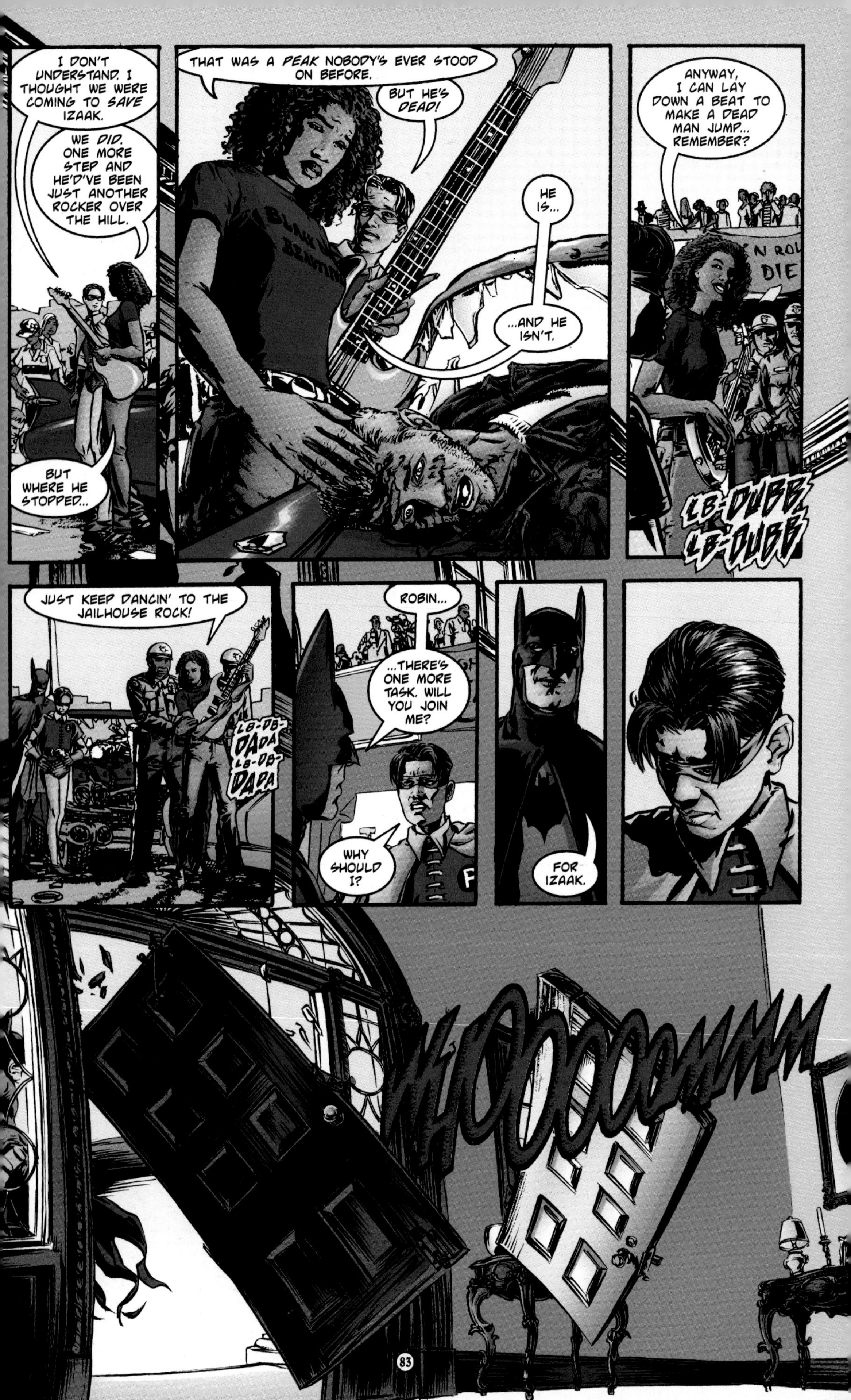

I DON'T UNDERSTAND. I THOUGHT WE WERE COMING TO SAVE IZAAK.
WE DID. ONE MORE STEP AND HE'D'VE BEEN JUST ANOTHER ROCKER OVER THE HILL.
BUT WHERE HE STOPPED...
THAT WAS A PEAK NOBODY'S EVER STOOD ON BEFORE.
BUT HE'S DEAD!
HE IS...
...AND HE ISN'T.
ANYWAY, I CAN LAY DOWN A BEAT TO MAKE A DEAD MAN JUMP... REMEMBER?
LB-DUBB LB-DUBB
JUST KEEP DANCIN' TO THE JAILHOUSE ROCK!
LB-DB-DADA LB-DB-DADA
ROBIN...
...THERE'S ONE MORE TASK. WILL YOU JOIN ME?
WHY SHOULD I?
FOR IZAAK.
WHOOOOOMMM

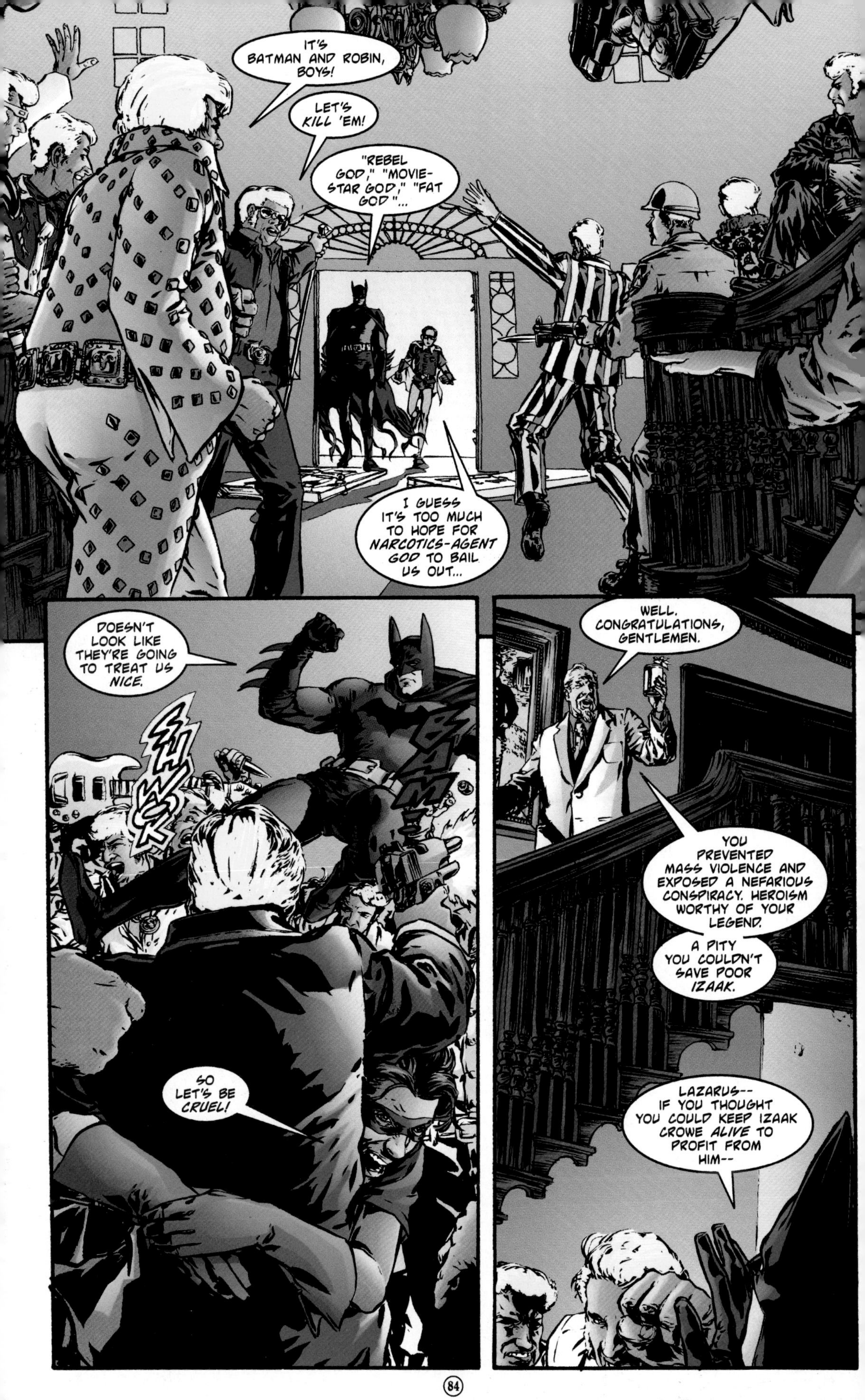
IT'S BATMAN AND ROBIN, BOYS!
LET'S KILL 'EM!
"REBEL GOD," "MOVIE-STAR GOD," "FAT GOD"...
I GUESS IT'S TOO MUCH TO HOPE FOR NARCOTICS-AGENT GOD TO BAIL US OUT...
DOESN'T LOOK LIKE THEY'RE GOING TO TREAT US NICE.
SHWOCK
BAMM
SO LET'S BE CRUEL!
WELL. CONGRATULATIONS, GENTLEMEN.
YOU PREVENTED MASS VIOLENCE AND EXPOSED A NEFARIOUS CONSPIRACY. HEROISM WORTHY OF YOUR LEGEND.
A PITY YOU COULDN'T SAVE POOR IZAAK.
LAZARUS-- IF YOU THOUGHT YOU COULD KEEP IZAAK CROWE ALIVE TO PROFIT FROM HIM--

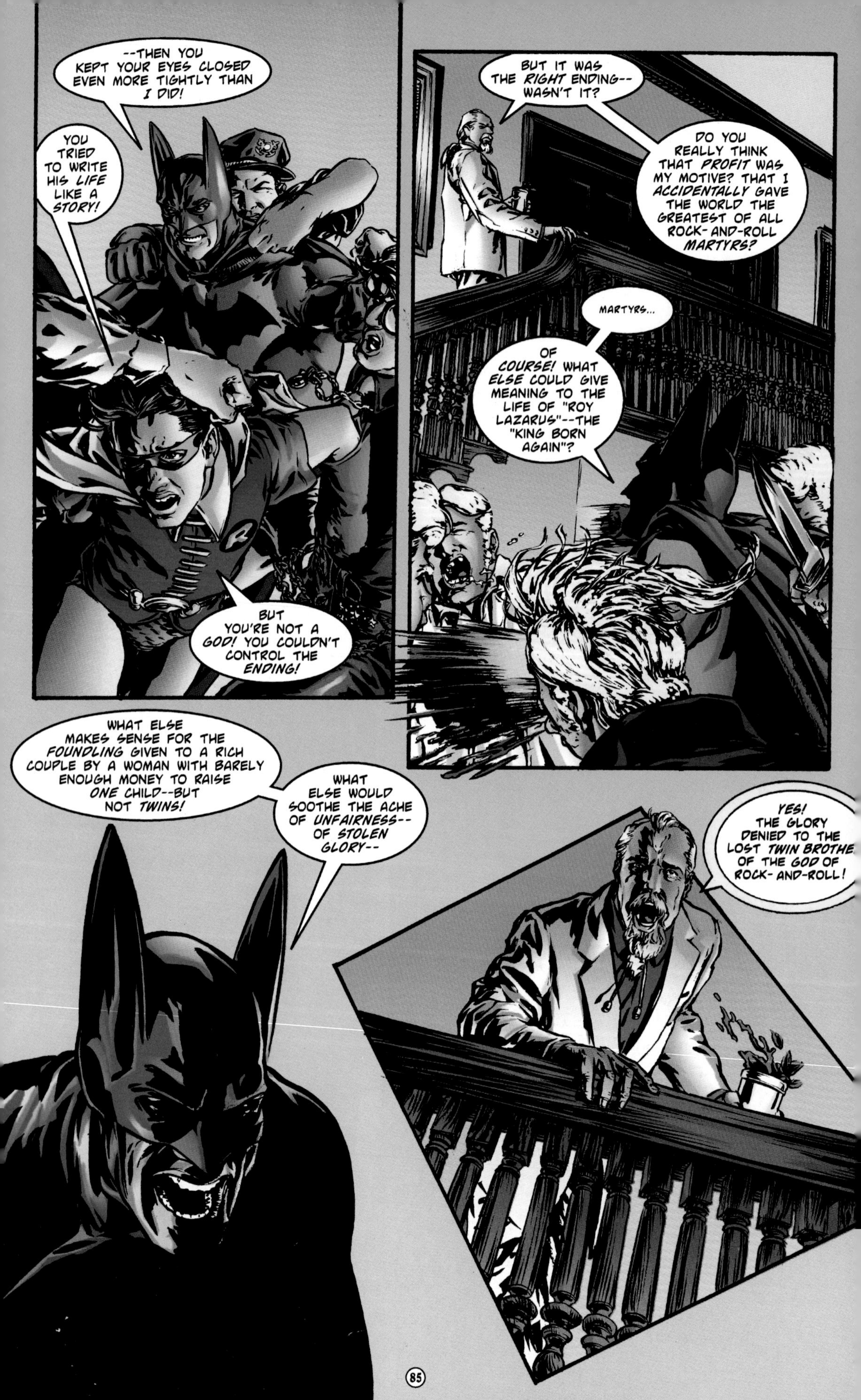
--THEN YOU KEPT YOUR EYES CLOSED EVEN MORE TIGHTLY THAN I DID!
YOU TRIED TO WRITE HIS LIFE LIKE A STORY!
BUT YOU'RE NOT A GOD! YOU COULDN'T CONTROL THE ENDING!
BUT IT WAS THE RIGHT ENDING--WASN'T IT?
DO YOU REALLY THINK THAT PROFIT WAS MY MOTIVE? THAT I ACCIDENTALLY GAVE THE WORLD THE GREATEST OF ALL ROCK-AND-ROLL MARTYRS?
MARTYRS...
OF COURSE! WHAT ELSE COULD GIVE MEANING TO THE LIFE OF "ROY LAZARUS"--THE "KING BORN AGAIN"?
WHAT ELSE MAKES SENSE FOR THE FOUNDLING GIVEN TO A RICH COUPLE BY A WOMAN WITH BARELY ENOUGH MONEY TO RAISE ONE CHILD--BUT NOT TWINS!
WHAT ELSE WOULD SOOTHE THE ACHE OF UNFAIRNESS--OF STOLEN GLORY--
YES! THE GLORY DENIED TO THE LOST TWIN BROTHE OF THE GOD OF ROCK-AND-ROLL!

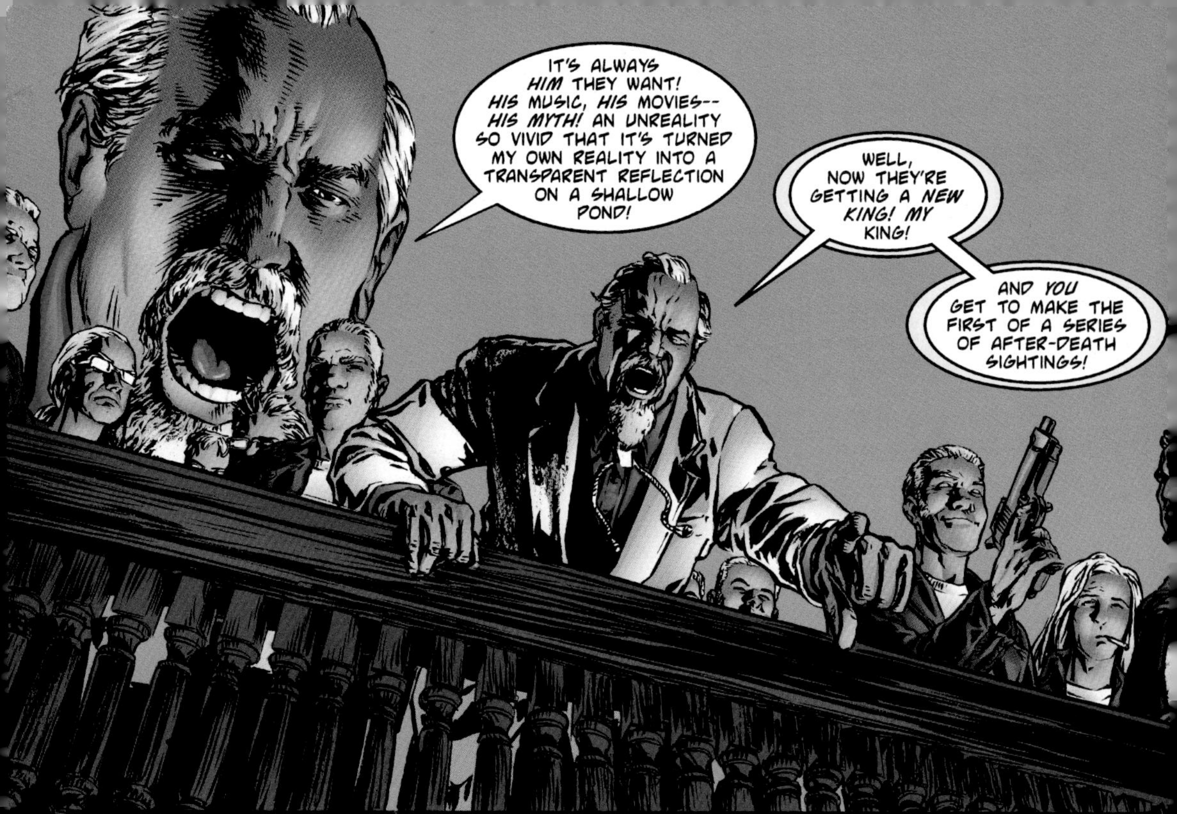
IT'S ALWAYS *HIM* THEY WANT! *HIS* MUSIC, *HIS* MOVIES-- *HIS MYTH!* AN UNREALITY SO VIVID THAT IT'S TURNED MY OWN REALITY INTO A TRANSPARENT REFLECTION ON A SHALLOW POND!
WELL, NOW THEY'RE GETTING A *NEW KING! MY* KING!
AND *YOU* GET TO MAKE THE FIRST OF A SERIES OF AFTER-DEATH SIGHTINGS!

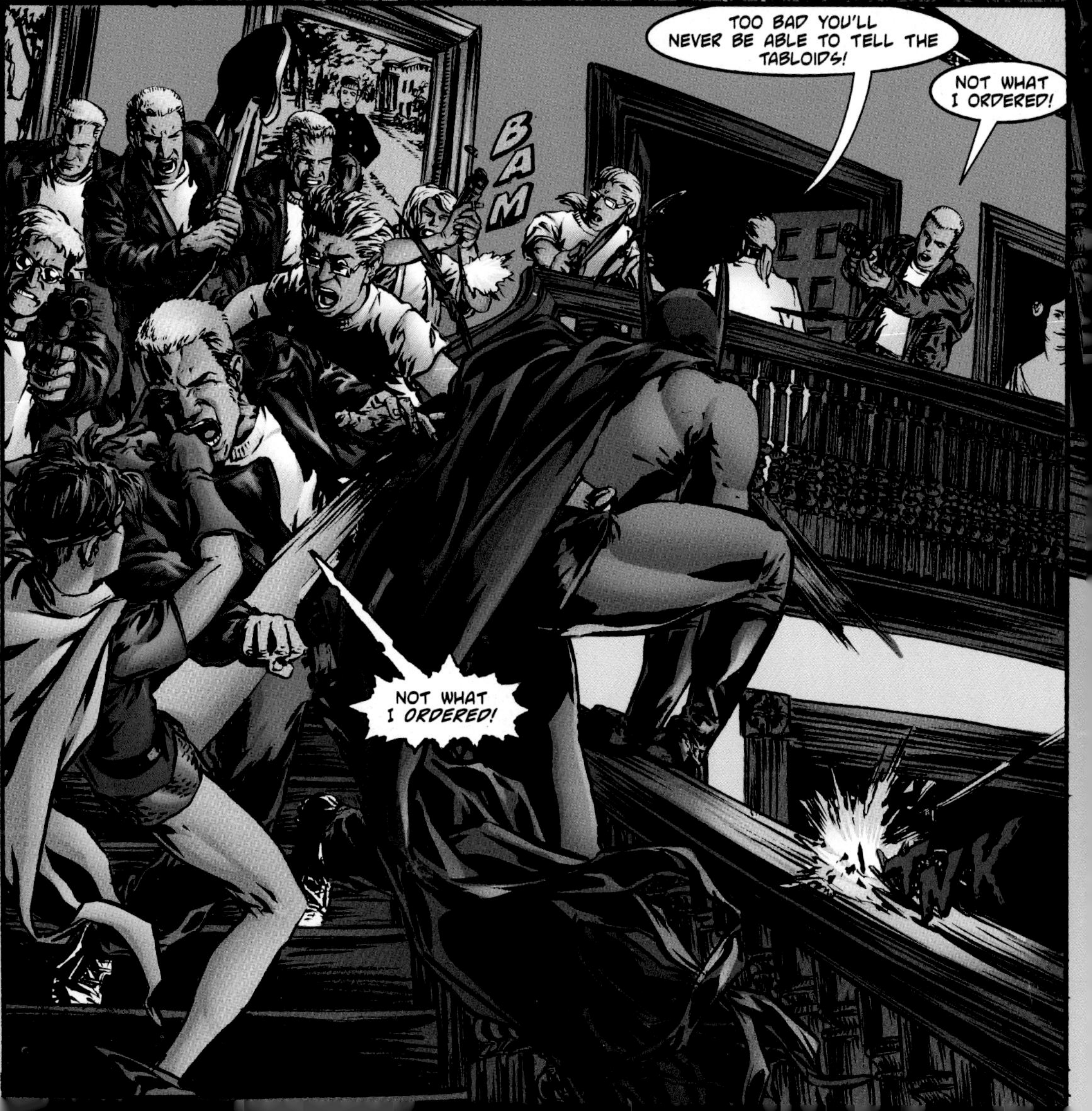
BAM
TOO BAD YOU'LL NEVER BE ABLE TO TELL THE TABLOIDS!
NOT WHAT I ORDERED!
NOT WHAT I *ORDERED!*

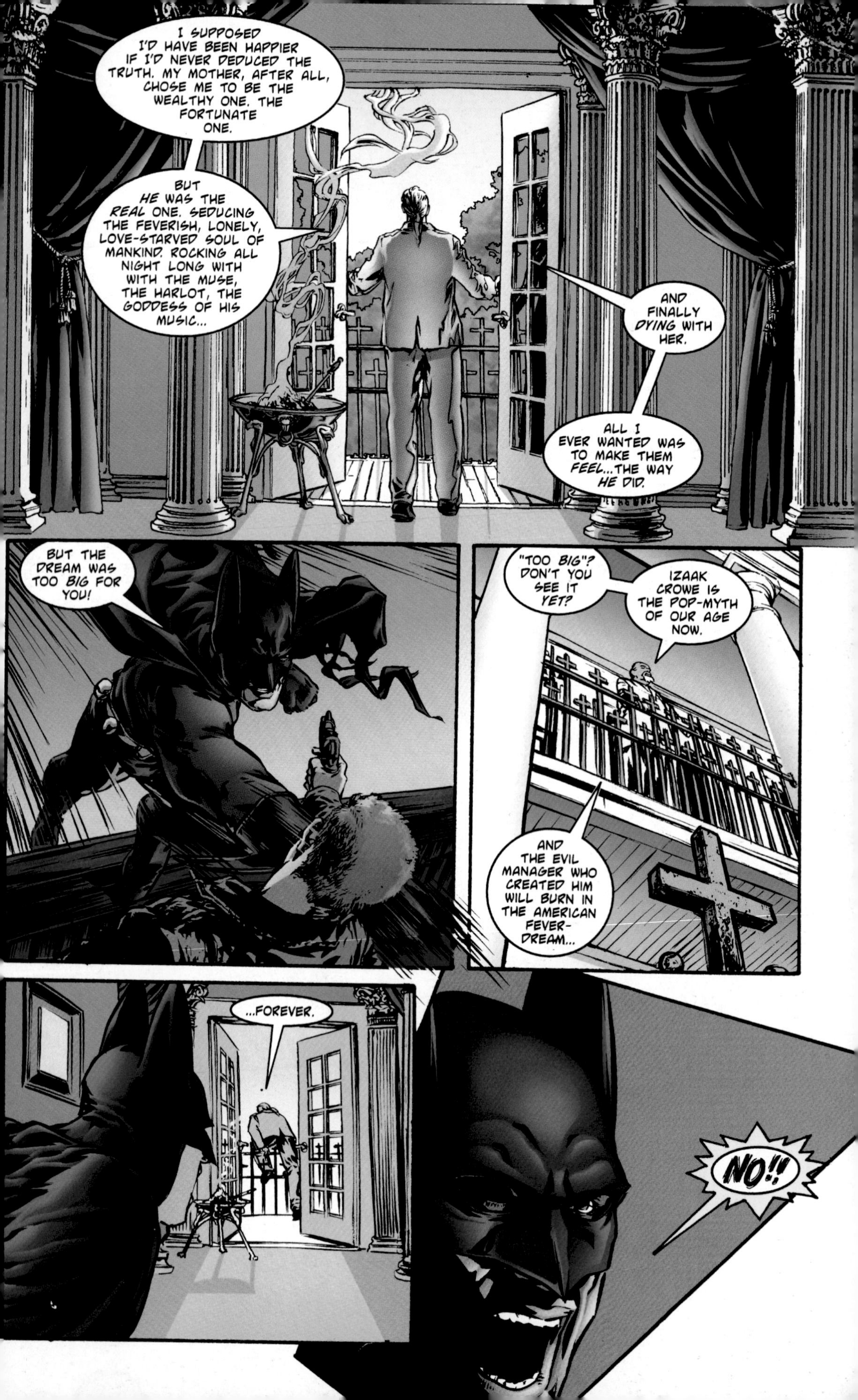
I SUPPOSED I'D HAVE BEEN HAPPIER IF I'D NEVER DEDUCED THE TRUTH. MY MOTHER, AFTER ALL, CHOSE ME TO BE THE WEALTHY ONE. THE FORTUNATE ONE.
BUT HE WAS THE REAL ONE. SEDUCING THE FEVERISH, LONELY, LOVE-STARVED SOUL OF MANKIND. ROCKING ALL NIGHT LONG WITH WITH THE MUSE, THE HARLOT, THE GODDESS OF HIS MUSIC...
AND FINALLY DYING WITH HER.
ALL I EVER WANTED WAS TO MAKE THEM FEEL...THE WAY HE DID.
BUT THE DREAM WAS TOO BIG FOR YOU!
"TOO BIG"? DON'T YOU SEE IT YET?
IZAAK CROWE IS THE POP-MYTH OF OUR AGE NOW.
AND THE EVIL MANAGER WHO CREATED HIM WILL BURN IN THE AMERICAN FEVER-DREAM...
...FOREVER.
NO!!

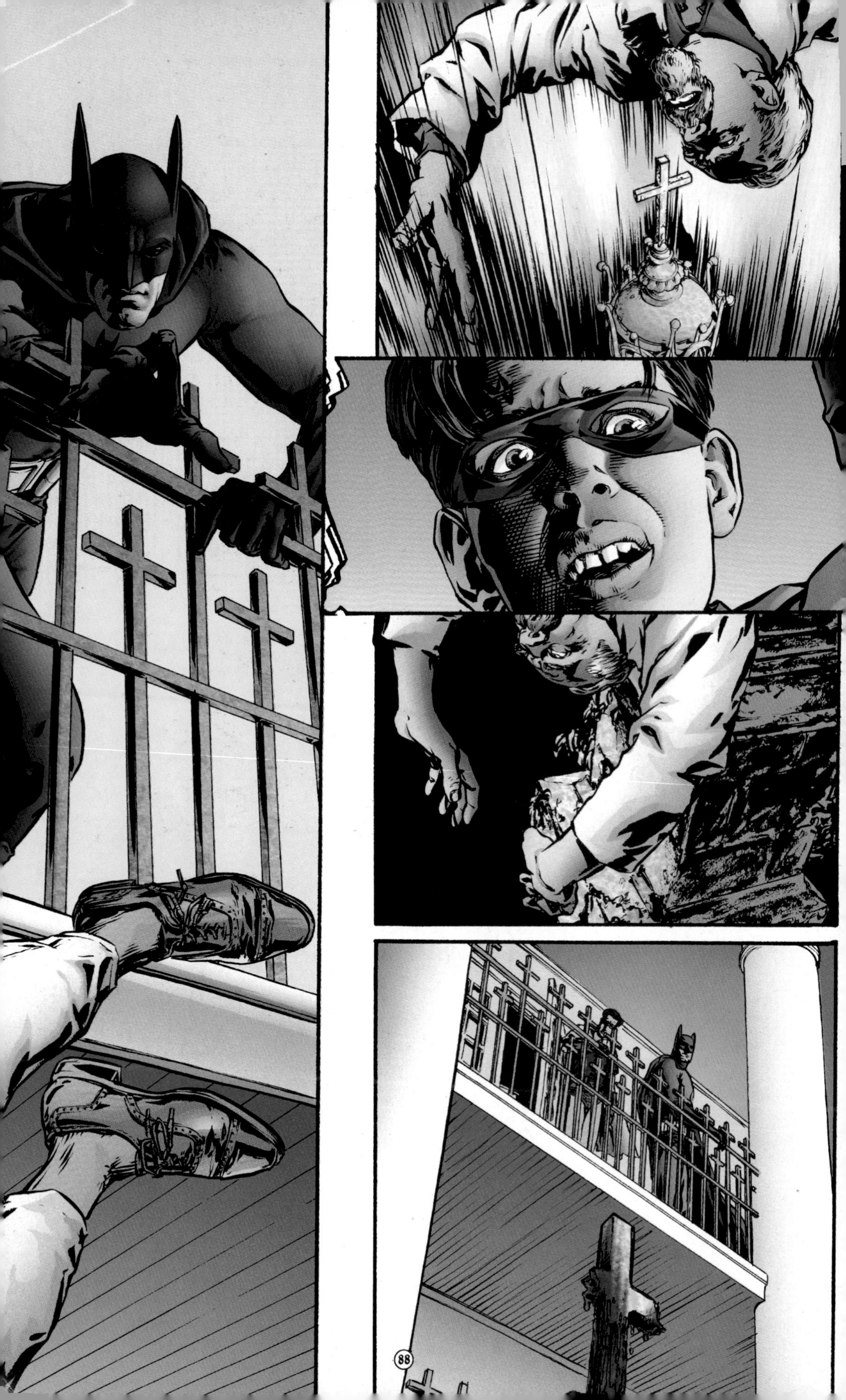

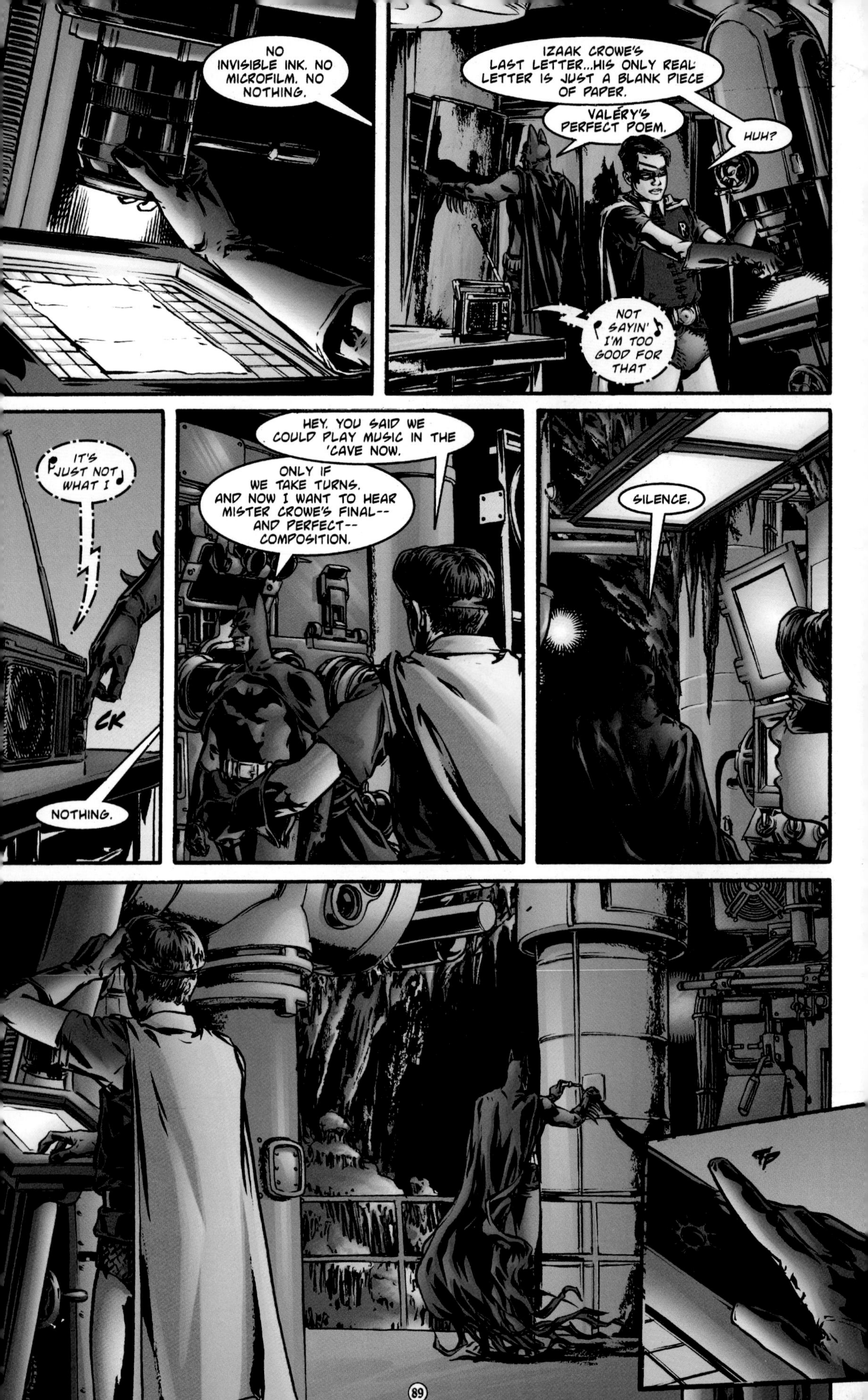
NO INVISIBLE INK. NO MICROFILM. NO NOTHING.
IZAAK CROWE'S LAST LETTER...HIS ONLY REAL LETTER IS JUST A BLANK PIECE OF PAPER.
VALÉRY'S PERFECT POEM.
HUH?
NOT SAYIN' I'M TOO GOOD FOR THAT
IT'S JUST NOT WHAT I
CK
NOTHING.
HEY. YOU SAID WE COULD PLAY MUSIC IN THE 'CAVE NOW.
ONLY IF WE TAKE TURNS. AND NOW I WANT TO HEAR MISTER CROWE'S FINAL-- AND PERFECT-- COMPOSITION.
SILENCE.

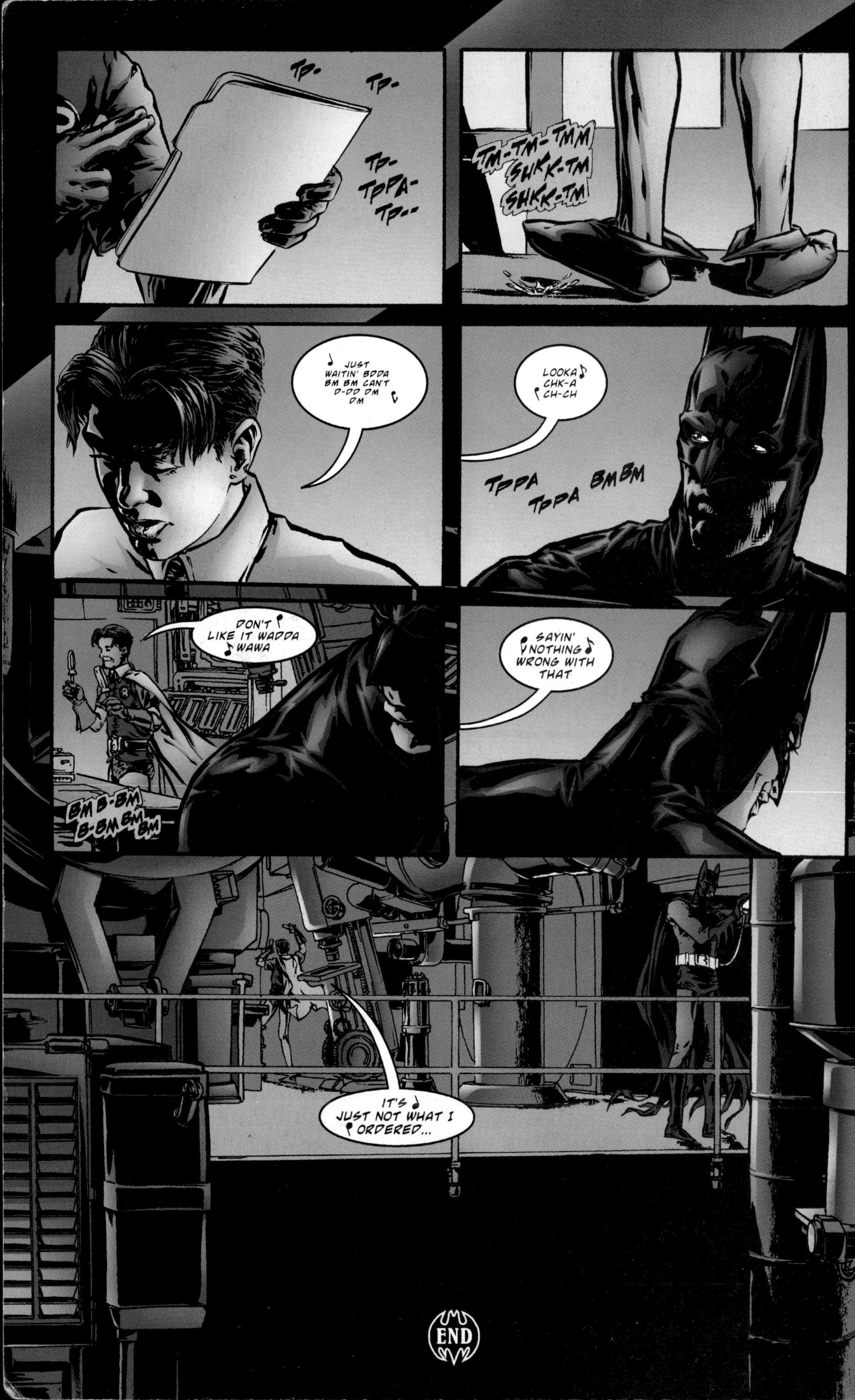
TP-
TP-
TP-
TPPA-
TP--
TM-TM-TMM
SHKK-TM
SHKK-TM
JUST WAITIN' BDDA BM BM CAN'T D-DD DM DM
LOOKA CHK-A CH-CH
TPPA
TPPA BMBM
DON'T LIKE IT WADDA WAWA
BMB-BM
B-BMBMBM
SAYIN' NOTHING WRONG WITH THAT
IT'S JUST NOT WHAT I ORDERED...
END

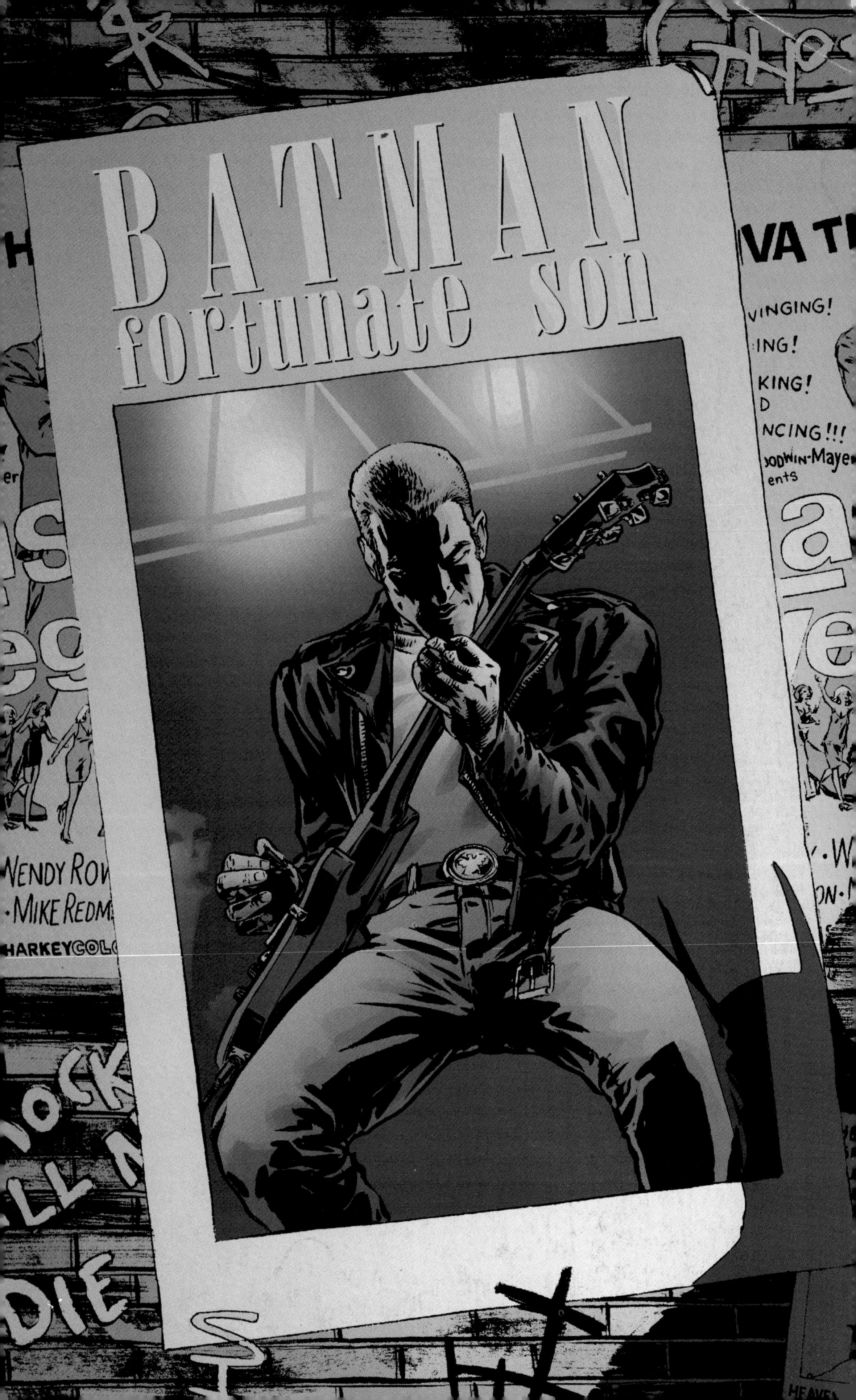
BATMAN
fortunate son

When Archie Goodwin first suggested a rock-and-roll Batman story, we responded with a ton of ideas but no central thread. Archie said, "Maybe there was a particular rock song or musician who meant something to Bruce Wayne when he was young. Maybe a song connected to a girl who meant something to him and he never saw again, or just a moment when Bruce could have changed things, could have been someone different." It was a simple idea, but it was exactly the piece we needed. With Batman's connection to the music established, his conflict with Robin was established, and then Robin's connection with Evangeline, Evangeline's true purpose, the emotional content of Izaak's mission and Roy's plans. A bunch of pop-culture conceits became a story.

Every time we worked with Archie it was the same: he wasted no time on superfluities and trivia, wasted no energy on power-tripping or second-guessing. He saw what was needed in the story and the art and gave us just enough to find it ourselves. Not surprisingly, neither of us has ever met anyone who understood how to tell a comics story as well as he did. For the last nine years of his life and career, Archie knew that he was dying of cancer. Happily for us, he chose to remain an editor until the end. As his strength failed and his hospital visits grew longer, he was forced to use his time more and more wisely. He was able to do so with complete grace, because his use of time was already wise. He allowed time for plot discussions, and for clear and specific notes; for talk about life and health and kids, and for jokes. Never for anything that he could trust to a writer or artist, or comfortably leave to fate.

Archie died after seeing only the first draft of this comic book's script. But we will always think of this as Archie's project as much as our own.

Gerard Jones

Gene Ha